Honors

2007 Poetry Collection

Published by
The America Library of Poetry
P.O. Box 978
Houlton, ME 04730
Website: www.libraryofpoetry.com
Email: generalinquiries@libraryofpoetry.com

Printed in the United States of America

THE AMERICA
LIBRARY OF POETRY

ISBN 10 Digit   0-9773662-2-7
ISBN 13 Digit   978-0-9773662-2-4

Contents

Poetry by Division

We Shall Never Forget

Many selections in this book are dedicated to you ...
the brave men and women of America's Armed Forces
who, since that fateful day on 9/11,
have tirelessly defended your country
and who, with the love and support of your families,
continue to proudly serve here at home
and in foreign lands around the world.
It is your sacrifice and dedication
which keeps the United States of America strong and free,
and for this, we are forever in your debt.
We want you to know that we are proud of you,
that we love you,
and that we pray for you ...
and for peace.

Foreword

There are two kinds of writers in the world.
There are those who write from experience,
and those who write from imagination.
The experienced, offer words that are a reflection of their lives.
The triumphs they have enjoyed, the heartaches they have endured;
all the things that have made them who they are,
they graciously share with us, as a way of sharing themselves,
and in doing so, give us, as readers, someone to whom we may relate,
as well as fresh new perspectives
on what may be our common circumstances in life.
From the imaginative, come all the wonderful things we have yet to experience;
from sights unseen, to sounds unheard.
They encourage us to explore the limitless possibilities of our dreams and fantasies,
and aid us in escaping, if only temporarily,
the confines of reality and the rules of society.
To each, we owe a debt of gratitude;
and rightfully so, as each provides a service of equal importance.
Yet, without the other, neither can be truly beneficial.
For instance, one may succeed in accumulating a lifetime of experience,
only to consider it all to have been predictable and unfulfilling,
if denied the chance to chase a dream or two along the way.
Just as those whose imaginations run away with them, never to return,
may find, that without solid footing in the real world, life in fantasyland is empty.
As you now embark, dear reader,
upon your journey through these words to remember,
you are about to be treated to both heartfelt tales of experience,
and captivating adventures of imagination.
It is our pleasure to present them for your enjoyment.
To our many authors,
who so proudly represent the two kinds of writers in the world,
we dedicate this book, and offer our sincere thanks;
for now, possibly more than ever,
the world needs you both.

Paul Wilson Charles
Editor

Editor's Choice Award

The Editor's Choice Award is presented to the author
who, more than any other, in our opinion,
demonstrates not only the solid fundamentals of creative writing,
but also the ability to illicit an emotional response
or provide a thought provoking body of work
in a manner which is both clear and concise.

You will find "Sonnet For Everyday People"
by Steven Abel
on page 217 of *With Honors*

Spirit of Education

For Outstanding Participation

2007

Virginia
Middle School
Bristol, Virginia

Presented to participating students and faculty
in recognition of your commitment
to literary excellence.

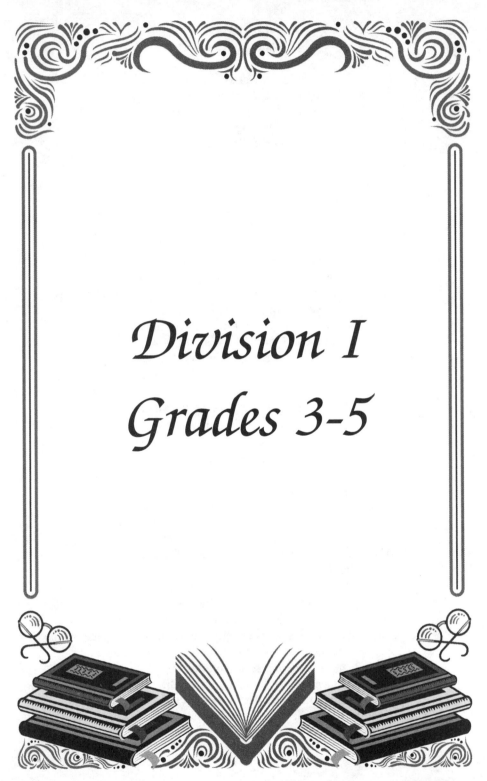

Division I
Grades 3-5

Orange
by Colin Alexander

Flickering as fast as bees' wings
Break dancing like a bull trying to buck off its rider
Bouncing off walls like crazy
In a zigzag
Like a bouncy ball that never stops

Egypt
by David Fain

Everywhere by brick, pyramids are being built
Millions of people are helping, there is much more to learn
In those pyramids, mummies are set to rest
Inside the sarcophagus, a mummy lies surrounded by jewels and gems
After all those years in Egypt, mummies go into the afterlife
And in the afterlife, they go through twelve dreadful gates
But the last one is the best one of all
Because it leaves you with no more fear

Beginning of the Championship
by Lauren Wangenstein

The gigantic field opened up to my eyes
Crisp air blowing my yellow jersey everywhere
Coaches putting up the enormous goals for the game
The field is being cleaned of the tons of garbage
So it doesn't affect us when we are playing
Teammates stretching on the sidelines
The other team boldly entering so we have a challenge
Some nervousness coming from my head
I'm worried that we will be in some competitive match
Cleats digging into the ground, readying our team for the battle
Mom giving me a hint to be aggressive and have fun!
Hot chocolate my mother gave me is warming me up and getting me pumped
People passing the round ball to each other to get warmed up
My team is gathering up to be told their positions
The excitement racing through my body like a race car
Racing to the race car as we start the game
That's what it's like at the beginning of a championship soccer game

I Am
by Nicole Leatherwood

I am a fairy that glistens in the sky
My mother is my faith; my father is my hope
I was born in another world
I live on a cloud
My best friend is a fairy like me because we like to imagine we fly
My enemy is dying because I love to live
I fear a lot of things because they're always there
I love the ocean because it's beautiful
I wish for everyone to be free

Green
by Fernando Ibanez

Flying leaves
The big and bright soccer field, the Green Bay Packers
The frogs going, "Ribbit, ribbit"
Juicy lemonade getting served in a cup, the cap of the green marker
Big and shiny green apples, bright lemons from a garden
Little green gummy bears, a green sweater that protects you from the cold weather
Long scissors, a green low rider
Green can start you out with a great April Fools'

Hawk
by Matthew Conlon

Soaring in the sky
Circling its prey to eat
Landing on branches

Hickory Dickory Dock
by Jakyra Cole

Hickory Dickory Dock
A mouse went up my sock
He wiggles his nose
He tickles my toes
Which gave me a great big shock

The Rat Brat
by Taylen Melcher

There was a rat
That was a brat
It could be a cat
But it was a rat
That ate a tart
That came from Bart
That lived in a box
That had chicken pox
That bought a train
That only ran in the rain

Spring
by Karaline Staggs

Spring is here again
Spring is the greatest season
Spring is fun with friends

I Am the Lemur
by Matthew Murphy

I am the lemur, small and quick; the way I look is very slick
I live in the jungle, tall and proud, where I look for food and swing around
I am an omnivore, small yet strong; I look for food all year long
I love to play and joke around; my eyes are yellow, small and round
Madagascar is great if you love trees; if you look carefully, you might see me!

Polar Bears
by Justin Niles

Polar bears, oh, so fluffy
Hearing the sound of the roaring winds
Eating all those frippery fins
Or diving in the deep blue
To catch a fish or maybe two
Seeing all the snow and ice
To the fish and seals, not very nice

Shoes
by Alex Howard

My shoes, black, white, dirty
My shoes, Vans, ripped, light
My shoes, holey, frayed laces, light, old
My shoes, comfortable

I Hate Poems
by Gavin Kelly

I can't write a poem
I can't write haiku
I can't write a limerick
I hate poems, I really do
I don't think they're funny
I don't think they're cool
I just do not like them
And I think they're really cruel
Poems are so boring
Poems are so bad
Poems are so evil
And they really make me mad
Poems aren't rewarding
Poems are no good
Poems might destroy us
And I really think they could
I write this message quickly
Before we humans fall
But sadly I wrote it in a form
That might destroy us all

Summer
by Hannah Duszynski

Summer days are here again
Hooray! Hooray! Hooray!
Time to swim, run and play!
Hooray! Hooray! Hooray!
I wish, I wish we never had to go back to school
Boo, boo, boo

What Is Green?
by Ryan Sleszynski

Green is an apple, it is really sweet but you can't eat it with your feet
Green is a lime with the juice over a mime
Green is the color of fresh grass but not the color of a rash
The sound of green is, "Swoosh! Swoosh!"
Green is a soccer field, green is an old man's shield
Green is a happy feeling; it reminds me of summer when the grass is green
Green is a bean, green is the outside of a watermelon, green is a crayon
It is a sick fish, green is the best!
Green ...

Lamp
by Brianna Smith

Lamp
Bright, tall
Lighting, shining, sparkling
Metal, plug, hard, plastic
Shadowing, brightening, glittering
Holdable, droppable
Flashlight

Pussy Willow
by Travis McQuade

Very soft leaves and
Stems that can grow very big
Buds that feel like soft skin

My Evil Prayers
by Austin Yeo

Once I was at a fair; I had an evil prayer
It was about a mad bear that tore out my brother's hair
Once I was at a fair; I had an evil prayer
It was about a giraffe's ridiculous fall because it was way too tall
Once I was at a fair; I had an evil prayer
It was about an ugly dog that looked like a very weird hog
Today was fun praying at the fair
But there is a fact today that I shall say amen to my evil prayers

The Blue Sky
by Trevor Dunn

The blue sky is wonderful with all its natural colors
With all its pink, blues and greens, hey don't forget the others
The sky is full of wondrous things, like birds that fly and soar
They are along the coast and in the sky and even on the shore
And in the sky there are tons of clouds, every day in every way
But not when you look down, I know they're up there today
All around the world is that big blue sky
If you take the time to look you'll find it's not a lie
Isn't the blue sky wonderful? Enjoy it until it says goodbye

Summer Fun
by Tyler Abbett

It is always pretty fun in the hot summer sun
We jump and play and fiddle all day
Maybe a dip in the pool
Oh, the water's really cool
After a long day of playing
Pretty soon I'm saying
It is pretty fun in the hot summer sun

Humans
by Aaron Chan

We are all humans
Living things, like the earth of the Earth
Not only are we growing together, we're also filled with talent
Everyone is special in a different way, and full of secrets and differences
You don't have to be the same, but it might be fun
Some people feel sad or happy sometimes
Different faces and languages too
It's sometimes great or may be cruel
We have different strengths and defenses, too
We all do things differently; you're not alone, no one is
'Cause people are all around you, so let's live
Peacefully together forever more

What Is Green?
by Casey Clifford

Green is the color of a Christmas tree
The color of the grass, money you pay a fee with
The color of an apple, the seaweed in the sea
The brother of green is blue, the color of a wrapper on your glue
Green is the leaves swaying in the summer, the leaves outside in the spring
Green is the color of happiness, the blanket you bring
The stem of a birthday flower, the color of an infection when you get a bee sting
The sound of green is, "Thump, thump, thump!"
A fish in tropical waters, the color of a slithering snake
A flower in a garden, the handle on a rake
Green ...

The Beautiful Night
by Danielle Roach

Night, night, night, what a wonderful night
It is the only thing I can't see in, but it is very shiny
It is a perfect night to be in
Fires and campers roasting their marshmallows under the big yellow moon
But it is only one night; the only night that is very bright
It's just one very bright night; it's just one very bright night
Night, night, night

Pickled Sister
by Madison Arrington

My sister just adores pickles
One day she turned into one and oh, believe me it wasn't fun
She turned into a pickled sister
And stuck to me like a blister
So my mom and dad thought it was okay to take her somewhere today
So we took her to the bowling alley and we sold her to a daddy
(For his dog's chew-toy and for $500.50)
This is my pickled, blistered, sticky sister
I wonder what she's doing now, hmm?

My Guardian Angel
by Victoria Ferme

My grandpa died when my mom was a kid
I heard he was a good singer
I also heard that his symbol is a butterfly that flows in the wind
I look up high and say, "Hello"
So I know he loves me very so

This Is the Fourth of July
by Tony Novotny

This is the Fourth of July
Kids on the street playing football
Fireworks bursting in the air like colorful bombs!
The neighbors are cheering for the fireworks
The cops come for the people setting them off
This is the Fourth of July
Shadows of kids tackling one another
A kid yells, "Hut 1, hut 2, set ... hike!"
A kid saying, "Ugh!" from being tackled really hard
When I play football, I am a volcano ready to erupt
This is the Fourth of July

It's Time To Rhyme
by Robert Bergmen

My teacher told me to not hit
So I didn't hit, I just slit
I am running in the yard
So I gave my dog a card
I am on top of the hill
So my mom can't find Bill
I am playing hide and seek
I accidentally broke the antique
I am a bird; I'm sitting on a log
Oh no, I can't see in the fog

Candy, Candy
by Nicky Ponce

Candy, candy is so sweet
Candy, candy what a treat
Do you like it?
Or like being fit?
It makes your teeth the color yellow
It makes your mother want to bellow
Brush your teeth and stop eating candy
And your life will be so dandy
Liking candy isn't bad
But after awhile you will be sad
The reason is because you will get fat
Very unlike a thin baseball bat
But still, candy is sweet
And it still is a treat

Sweet Dreams
by Emily Feigenbaum

One day you have a dream of going to a place made of ice cream
There is a chocolate river full of sweetness and life
You slice a cupcake with a sugar knife
As you sit down on a candy chair, you feel a breeze out of nowhere
This breeze takes you back home
But you forgot one thing, your ice cream cone!

The Husky
by Thomas Lehecka

Snowy mountain top
Siberian Husky's fur blows in the breeze
Aqua eyes pierce the light, winter mist
Elegantly dancing across the sky
He sprints across a silver path
His howl is heard everywhere
His coat shines like the night moon
As he cuddles up with his family to get some rest
His fur so soft and well groomed
Commander of the mountains

There Once Was a Boy From Hong Kong
by D.J. Estrada

There once was a boy from Hong Kong
He liked to play the gong
Then he met a girl named May
She saw the gong and threw it away
Now all he could do was sing a song

Trees
by Alexandria Adams

Trees are big and small
Trees are fun to play on
Trees are magnificent in every way
Let's go out and play

Ode To My Mother
by Corinne Caviggiola

Ode to my mother, a darling she
When I wake up, you are the first face I see
When things don't go our way
"It's okay," is all you will say
You love me when I am sick
You'll scream if I ever get a tick
Keep up your work
For you will not regret it

Chocolate Fondue
by Mackenzie Waugh

Melting pot of chocolate, yummy, yummy
So delicious, yet never nutritious
It is yummy, yummy in my tummy
Dipping strawberries is so delicious
At least the berries are nutritious
But don't eat too many, you will get sick
But don't cry, the ick will never stick

The Traveler
by Chris Swanner

There once was a traveler who had to unraveler
One of the presents he got; what he found was a big, black yacht!
So he sailed to paradise and to his surprise
When he got there, he didn't care; he just wanted to go home
So he sailed back to the big city; he wasn't looking very pretty
He hadn't shaved in weeks; he hadn't washed his cheeks
He needed a bath because he smelled like a rat
So he got in the tub and started to scrub
He was happy to be home

Angel From Above
by Jenna Wernke

A bright light catches my eye
A shining star up in the sky
I think of you each time I see
A beautiful light shining down on me
The clouds open for you to shine
My delicate angel to send me a sign
I know you're still there each day and each night
So that is why this poem I write
I send my love from me to you
I miss you, I miss you, yes I do

Stone Swan
by Logan White

Sitting next to cement cattails, the stone swan is carved into a pavilion
Where it is a clone to the real beauty of the snow colored bird
With no feeling but sorrow, for like Pinocchio, it will never be real

Sara
by Amber Roberson

She wasn't just a person; she was a friend
She was like a butterfly, always with me when I needed her
I'll never forget her smile, but most of all
I'll never forget the day she flew up to Heaven

School
by Cody Alan Kellar

My true name is Cody; my family calls me Code
My fifth grade teacher piles us up with homework that's quite a heavy load
Our teacher always wants us to do our best
But I find it difficult to keep up with the rest
I would love to remain a young kid, always at play
Riding bikes and jumping rope would really make my day
They tell us we need an education to get a job
So I won't have to work with the mob
So always do your best in school
You don't want to look like a fool

Isla Cruisa
by Bailey Grayson

If you're feeling blue, go talk to bamboo and there is a pirate waiting
He'll say, "Welcome aboard, there is much to be explored on Isla Cruisa"
So they'll grab you and wrestle you until you're in the bag
And they'll take you aboard and get the rum and the pirate suit
So they'll take you out of the bag, they'll pamble and scramble you into the suit
And they'll hand you the rum and say you're dumb
They'll say land and you'll find the treasure
And that's what you do if you're feeling blue; Isla Cruisa is still waiting for you!

Open Field
by Kyle Endlekofer

Birds flying in the sky, singing songs
The wind blowing silently like the water when the tide is low
A little pond where ducks swim about ...
Ducks quacking, ducks quacking, ducks quacking
The forest trees are moving slowly
The leaves are rustling
The trees hold a dark shadow covering the field, like a blanket to a baby
Ducks quacking, ducks quacking, ducks quacking
The water in the pond is motionless
The shadow of the birds flying in the sky appears overhead
The sun is setting behind the trees
Ducks quacking, ducks quacking, ducks quacking

Summertime
by Haleigh Taylor

Summertime is here; it's my favorite time of year
As the waves splash, and sandcastles crash
Summertime is here
Under the sunshine, we waste our time
As I eat my ice cream, I wonder if it's a dream
Summertime is here
As the wind blows, no one knows
When Mother Nature will call for the leaves to fall
Then summertime will be over, oh dear!

What Is Red?
by Nick Palmieri

Red is paper after looking on a screen
Red Jell-O that is mellow; it is people being mean
Red is squishy Jell-O
Red is Kool-Aid
Red is a color that you have seen
Red is bright like when birds take flight
Red is like an attack; it is the opposite of black
Red is a party cup, the red sunrays are up; it's a clear clipboard
Red is a marker and a balloon, you should like it soon

A Dream
by Madeline Sytsma

A dream is a peaceful thing
It is something that you get when you are sound asleep
In your wonderful bed, in a dream you can venture very far
To places that you've never been, up to a star!
Dreams are very soothing for when you're in distress
Yes, dreams are very wonderful for you and I to see!
Any type of dream is nice except for the bad
Daydreams, night dreams, any type at all!

I'm Lonely In a City
by Eileen Chou

I'm lonely in a city
Just left here to die, I wish someone could help me
But all I can do is cry, I'm lonely in a city
A tsunami is coming my way
All that is left is my soul here today

Mrs. Snoopy
by Tyler Crane

We have a teacher
Her name is Mrs. Snoopy
She is very loopy
Everybody in the school said she is goopy!

Clouds
by Kevin McCarthy

Cloud one, cloud two, cloud three
All are white in the big, big sky
They are so mighty
And sometimes look funny
Like a bunny

Manatees
by Shelby Brankle

Manatees
Calm, happy
Always swimming around
Eating, drinking, sleeping, breathing
Sea cow, big, dazzling, it's dying out
Moving, grazing, swimming, swaying
Mermaid, gray, blue, we're killing it
Wondering wishing, thinking, spinning
Manatees

Leaf Bare
by Leah Zetterlund

It was getting colder; fall was approaching
The little brown leaf was being shaken by the cold wind of the approaching fall
He was tossing and shaking through a day and a night
Then a freezing dawn light glowed and at that same instant he had to let go
Now the little brown leaf was away from home
The wind picked him up, carrying him far; now he was soaring through the forest
The little brown leaf looked down on the forest
He saw a squirrel digging up acorns it had buried
He drifted beyond the forest to a meadow where he saw a deer grazing freely
He came to a stream that led to a pond; the little brown leaf looked at the pond
And there he saw a raccoon eating small fish it had caught
Now the little brown leaf floated to the ground
Where the last seed he was carrying rooted
And all around he saw other leaves falling to the ground

Dogs
by Ingrid Angulo

They aren't really perfect with that horrible, smelly smell
The furry ones shed tons of fur on your perfect couches and carpets
They bark and yelp all night
If the ball of fur is big or small, it doesn't matter
They are still downright annoying at times!
Once they bite you, you feel like it's all over
When you take them on walks they end up taking you on walks
I'm warning you, don't get the ball of fur they call a dog!

Red
by Lorna Gavin

Flames charging after me, blood streaming down my hurt arm
Hair of a freckled girl, V8 getting poured in an iced glass
Christmas songs sung in harmony, an apple crunching in my watery mouth
A strawberry freshly washed, spicy chile powder with cucumbers
A freshly cut tomato, Mexico's humid desert
A warm shower after going out in the snow, an alarm clock ringing wildly
Red can get my dreams rock'n!

Football
by Cobi Rose

There once was a boy who played football
He saw the football
He kicked the football
He liked kicking the football

Callie
by Sarah Spencer

She was young, then she was old, but she was always bold
She was cute and always getting into Daddy's suits
If only she could still play, but she's in Heaven today
She died of old age; that filled me with rage
Because I loved her so
My darling cat, I want her back
Because I loved her more than the sun and the seashore
My darling cat, I want her back
Because I loved her so

The Beautiful Garden
by Paul Root

There are beautiful red and white roses
Purple tulips, butter yellow lilies, and blue sea holly
There are birds chirping, and leaves rustling
An oak tree slowly sways in the breeze
It is very quiet ...
The day is sunny and bright
There is fresh dew on the roses
The sky is baby blue, filled with white, puffy clouds
The tulips are blooming in the morning
And the dew on the flowers is gleaming in the golden sun
It is very quiet ...
The leaves around me are dark green
And I am walking on a square shaped path
But when I come to this same garden the next day ...
It is not there
It must be magic
It is very quiet ...

What Is Green?
by Lauren DePol

Green is the color of grass
Green is St. Patrick's Day; clovers are green
When I see green, I think of "go"
Christmas trees are green
Grapes are green, maybe even apples
Green is the sound of leaves dancing in the wind
Springtime begins with green
Grass getting greener, plants growing, trees blooming
Money is green!
Green is spring and autumn; I love green!
Red and green are Christmas colors
Green and yellow are best friends
Green is the fourth color in the rainbow
Frogs can be green; green is land!

The City
by Amanda Graziano

Buildings, plays, Central Park, churches
Taxis, traffic, crowded people and crowded places
Horns honking because of traffic, kids climbing in Central Park
At Christmas time, people walking down the lit-up streets singing carols
Everything is so exciting, the interesting artifacts in the Museum of Natural History
Everyone is walking closely, crowded together, to get from place to place
The stars in the Broadway plays, the fun of the city

The Tap Dance
by Kate Stanko

A soft tap of rain
The pitter patter of its dance
It is a tap dance
Pit, pat, pit, is its rhythm on my roof
A dance of drops

The Shoe Kristen-Two
by Megan Holbrook and Kyleigh Cooper

There was a very nice shoe named Kristen-Two
Her owner left her in the church on the pew
She was really sad so she sang the blues

What Is Turquoise?
by Madeline Lee

Turquoise is like a beautiful sky
With a big white cloud up very high
It is a cool day in the summer
Turquoise is tasty
Making beautiful rainbows, now don't be hasty
Turquoise is a beautiful color
Turquoise is like a blue bay on a warm beach
Making a huge spray; it is so wonderful
Turquoise is like tasty cotton candy with M&M's
It's quite dandy to have a color like you
Turquoise is an ocean with a nice beach
It will make a devotion to you and me
Turquoise is like a fish swimming in the water
Granting every wish; what a beautiful sight
Turquoise smells like flowers with a very nice home
It gets all the showers because it is a beautiful turquoise

Joined Hearts
by Hannah Gately

Joined hearts together, open the stage curtains wide
The winged music floats across the stage to my ears
And starts my heart thundering for you
And finally, you are there, glowing like a god
Brighter than the spotlight shining on you; dance for me, dance for me my darling!
Shining brightly you eclipse the brilliance of the sun
Jealous the sun burns brighter, trying to outshine perfect you
Oh ... I long to be your source of energy
Your favorite strawberry juice is what I long to be
I wish to refill and enrich you after you finish dancing

Who Am I?
by Troy Myers

There are different kinds of me
When I grow up I will be four feet in length
I have texture on my body
I am endangered
I make a nest
I live in the sea or land
I have a shell
I am green
Who am I?

What Is Green?
by Katelyn Molloy

Green is a leaf, it is the grass, it is land, Jell-O is the color green
Green is a four-leaf clover and a Christmas tree
In a rainbow, green comes after yellow
A grape is green, green is a pepper, a mint, and a lollypop
Money is green, the season of green is spring
The feeling of green is happy and brave
Green speckles falling from trees can be heard dancing in the wind
Green's older brother is blue, and younger is yellow

Inside a House
by Joseph Damiano

Inside a house you may find a night light
And the nice people that live there when they go to sleep
If you're lucky, Mrs. Theisen or Mrs. Cimino might live there
You may find a bed or more and you may find windows or more than one
You may also find a door or two and maybe more
You will find a roof and some walls
You may find some homework and you may find a report card

Little Monkey
by Abigail Kirchner

Little monkey
Swinging from tree to tree
Eating bananas
Tails flying
Little, big, crazy
Coconuts falling
Sitting on a banana tree
Dropping the peels on the ground
Favorite animal
Big monkey

What Is Red?
by Steven Genova

Red is my favorite color; it reminds me of things I like
Apples, watermelon, Santa, strawberries and a shiny new bike
Red is the hot, summer sun when there are no clouds in the sky
Red is the color of a delicious, warm, cherry pie
Red is the stripes on the flag; our flag is Red, White and Blue
My basketball sneakers are red; my mom calls me 'Mr. Red Shoes'
Red is the color of a cardinal singing outside my room
Red is for a stick of dynamite, boom, boom, boom!
Red is a color for holidays, especially Valentine's Day!
Red is for some teams I like, USC, Ohio State and BC on game day
Red ...

Blue
by Gabrielle Castilletti

I'm feeling blue
Yes, it's true because I have the flu
My brother has it too
Yes, it's true
My mother's friend Sisy Lou
Came to check on us, then she got it too
Yes, it's true!

What Is Lavender?
by Jillian Prystupa

Lavender is a wonderful feeling
It is bright and nice; it can be the color of the ceiling
Lavender is such a beautiful color; lavender is the color of flowers
It can be the day or the weeks, hours
Or if you please, just the night, it can be the color of a lollipop
It can be anything you desire, maybe a glass teapot
It is definitely great; it is a very good smell
So very perfect, can you tell?
Nothing is better; lavender is a soft sound
You can barely notice, like sand piling on a mound
I love it so much; it has a touch like a rocking chair
So soft and wonderful like a teddy bear
A wonderful touch, it is delicious, so sweet
People are vicious to eat it; it looks very great
It is bright, yet dark; 10 as the best it is number 8
It is the best in the world; I love it so
A great color, it makes me glow
It is soft, sweet and wonderful

How Are You Feeling?
by Sophia Lopez

Curious is white like a blank piece of paper when I have nothing to do but draw
It walks in through my mind
It reminds me of things I have asked my hard-working parents
It makes me feel weird or like a computer that just won't work
It makes me want to know what the world will end up like

City
by Courtney Hickey

Streets as large as the ocean; cars vrooming and beeping
People in a hurry as if there is a world race
Shadows surrounding people and buildings
Chatters ... honks ... beeps ... vrooms ...
Fast and exciting; happy, terrific, and loud
Dark, tall buildings; many places to go
Large city lights; my favorite place, the city

What Is Red?
by Stephanie Catoggio

Red is like cherries
When they glisten and gleam they are like berries
When they are ripe and ready the cherry's taste is awesome and sweet
They really don't smell like rotting feet
Red is like a fruit filled cart
There are many fruits in it; some of the fruits are the color of the heart
Cherries feel soft and sweet
They do not have the feel of feet

Winter Snow Falls
by Kathy Yeung

Winter snow falls
When you're at the mall you see the snow that is as white is a dove
You feel warmth when you're back at your house
The snow falls in the dark of December
In the dark of December, the snow falls
The trees are white when there is light
And the snow falls in the dark of December

The Sea
by Mariah Anton

Out here on the sea, on the sapphire sea
The galloping waves rush by, they seem to dance on the surface
A bright light warms your face, it is the lighthouse standing tall
Proud of its stripes and perfect straight sides
The sunset breaks through the misty sky
The sea begins to calm as night drifts on the pitch black water
The sky darkens, the stars brighten up like balls of fire
The night sky looks like a canvas, a painting
The sea is a dancer, it jumps from the depths, it leaps to the sky
The graceful sea is like a ballerina performing in the spotlight
Precise, the sea, my friend

Two Brother Dragons
by Clayton Cain

There once was a dragon so handsome and smart
He let people go free for he had a big heart
But his big, mean brother who lived deep in a cave
Always found people for him to crave
He ate them for lunch with a side of ale
He picked his teeth with his big, sharp nail
The big brother explained to his brother
That it filled him with laughter
They both agreed on the comment, and lived happily ever after

Autumn
by Cedric Cunningham

I see lots of trees
I can feel the windy breeze
Birds fly south in the sky
All the leaves crumble and die

Halloween
by Danielle Mattfeld

The leaves saying crackle, crackle
Different creatures surround me
The taste of flavored lip balm, too
When it gets windy the aroma of fresh pumpkin pie filling the room
Touching the hard and soft candy in my hand

Dreams
by Eric Cunningham

Every night, I lay and dream, dreaming of you and me
One day being together in harmony and in peace
The last time we spoke, I gave you a token of my gratitude for being there for me
You were there in times of joy and times of sorrow
When I was weak, you made me strong; in my time of need, you were there for me
You were there when I was born; you were there when I was torn
You carried a cross heavier than any human being could bear
I truly miss you everyday and every night; as a way to ease the pain, I lay at night
Dreaming of you and me and the way things used to be

What Is Purple?
by John Dragonetti

Purple is a grape or a plum that is tasty to eat, yum, yum!
Purple is the grandmother to pink and is more popular than you think
Purple is the color of my new t-shirt, and it even looks good on my sister's skirt
And a purple bruise that you wish you can lose
Purple is a feeling, a definite pout that is never left out
Violets blooming in the spring is a magnificent thing
Purple veils can be seen; some ladies even purple their fingernails
Purple is the color in the spring; that is a beautiful thing
Purple is a sweet candy that is very dandy
Purple can be seen after the rain, in an arch and through a windowpane!

A Frog In the Fog
by Kathy Jenkins

There once was a frog who got lost in the fog
He stood on a ball, and had a great fall
He fell to the river; it made his liver quiver
The river narrowed to a creek; the creek was named after a Greek
He jumped to a lily pad, and the frog named it Chad
There was his home, and he yelled, "My comb!"
Just then a fish said, "Hi," and a bird said, "My, my"
The fog, finally gone; he had been out since dawn!

Hug Bug
by Zack McNulty

There's a hug bug in my mug, mug
I tug and tug, but hug bug won't come out
It's like he's stuck in a whale's spout
I pout and pout, but he won't come out, out
So I try to make him go, so I cry and cry
And with a sigh, he leaves my mug without a tug, tug
He sighed and said, "Bye"
And that hug bug left only mug, mug with one goodbye, nice guy

What Is Yellow?
by Heather Price

Yellow is sour in the midnight hour
Yellow is the sunshine, light and thin; warm as a muffin on your skin
Yellow are the stars, Jupiter, Venus, Saturn and Mars
Yellow is a ring; yellow is a very beautiful thing
Yellow is a feeling rather sweet
Yellow is a fish that lives its life on a crystal dish
Yellow is a lion on the grassy plains of Africa's mane
I was once told that a color is yellow ...

My Favorite Place
by Hannah Rogers

My favorite place is the ocean, it swifts and it swivels
Fish, dolphins, sharks and whales living everywhere in it
Creatures so unique, it's what makes them interesting
I swim and jump in the waves, then get wrapped in my towel ready to go home
The ocean will wait for me until tomorrow and I will be there

Snow's Here
by Seth Tocco

It's cold outside, the wind chill's frozen
I like to play in the snow a dozen
People bundled, people cold
People say there's lots of colds
People here, people there
People, people everywhere
Hot chocolate is warm, and so am I
So, drink some with marshmallows inside
People say it's so delighting
Sleds falling, children gnawing
People say the snow has fallen
Snow is here, I know it is
People say there are lots of cold winds

Dreams
by Kayla Chambers

Dreams can be good, dreams can be bad
But all dreams have a purpose just like all of us in the world
Some of us may not think we're special but we really are
Now we may not be rich, we may not be poor
But if we all follow our dreams, we may even get to be president someday

The Jungle
by Rachel Meeks

The jungle is green
And easy to be seen
Animals are wild
The temperature is mild
In the jungle you better
Pack a healthy lunch in a sack
So when you cross a hungry tiger you will not be an appetizer
If you see a mama elephant
Be sure to sing a song of triumph
In the jungle you better creep because all the animals are asleep
The jungle is peaceful to me, if you go there you will see

Bionic Bunny
by Robert A.C. Martin

Bionic Bunny, Bionic Bunny, Bionic Bunny
Here he comes flying through the air
He can shoot lightning strikes from his hair
If he sees a criminal he's sure to get the punch
With Bionic Bunny gathering them by the bunch
Harry the Horse, Bionic Bunny will get him by the ear
Danger Dog, that's the end of his career
Sabotage Sheep, he's sure to be sheared
And if you're afraid, don't worry, 'cause Bionic Bunny is near

My Great Grandpa
by Alora Swafford

My heart is broken, my tears are running down my cheeks
My great grandpa has died today
He used to have a heart warming smile, he remembered me every day
But when he got sick he forgot me, I felt like he was slipping away
Every day he got worse, he didn't remember his family, not even his son
He died that night, sitting, holding my great grandma's hand
He died peacefully where he loved it most
He is sitting in his arm chair, he's holding his wife's hand
My memories of him are safe in my heart
And the thing I remember him by, is playing with me every day and every night

I Am
by Danielle Schwarz

I am a carefree girl who loves animals
I wonder if there are any new animals nobody knows about
I hear quacks and barks
I see people riding horses
I want to race horses
I am a carefree girl that loves animals
I pretend like I live in a house with five dogs, five cats, and five chinchillas
I feel like I could understand animals
I touch eagle's wings
I worry about my favorite animals getting extinct
I cry when I find out that an animal died
I am a carefree girl who loves animals
I understand that all living creatures die
I say you can save extinct animals
I dream that I can have one of each animal as my own
I try to make sure people don't kill animals
I hope that one day all animals could live together in peace
I am a carefree girl that loves animals

Moon
by Sam Griffin

Oh moon, sister of the sun
You glow in the night sky
You hang with the stars
You sing with the sun
Goddess of night
You light the lonely darkness

Jazlyn
by Alyssa Richards

She is my sister, dressed in green
Sometimes she can be very mean
Under that blond hair she can be smart
She's an A student; that's only part
She's not an angel; she's not a devil
She's just trying to be at my level
She's eight years old and she is my gold
I love my sister and that will never get old

The Octopus
by Emily Tomkiewicz

Eight legs awaking, stretching, having fun
Deep down where there's no sun
Catching crab, almost done
Crab for dinner yum, yum, yum
Swimming up to the sun to say hi to your friend fish
Promising you won't put him on your dish
Spin down to the bottom where there's no sun
Wave good night and tomorrow don't be a bum
Get up and have some fun
Turning, churning in the sand
Listening to the new mermaid band
It goes bong, hong, dong
All night long

Mother Nature
by Stella Blue Porzungolo

I am Mother Nature, kind and wise
My eyes are the clouds whose cries are rain
Don't pollute the air or my eyes will be in vain
I am Mother Nature, mayor of the green layers
Breathe in that fresh air, those are my perfumes
If you pollute it with gas it would just become a stinky fuel
Look at those beautiful trees sprouting into the air
Those trees are my hair; do not cut them down or I would be bald
And that is not a pretty sight; those daisies, tulips and pretty roses
Are my stubby finger less, the ocean is my mouth that opens really wide
Please do not dump any scraps in my mouth or then I will lie on my side and die
Other odds like berries, tomatoes and sprouting fruit
And veggies are jewels on my jewelry; necklaces, earrings and rings galore
Diamonds are a girl's best friend, even for Mother Nature
Mother Nature is just my formal name, you can call me Nanny
I look after every living thing on Earth from the plants
To a great blue whale under the sea; they are my children
So be careful to only kill what you need, I will have no children
I am Mother Nature, be kind to me

Newborn Baby
by Amanda Marcinek

Newborn baby is right in mother's arms
Beautiful sights in your baby's big, blue eyes
Crying and screaming but we get used to it
Loving and caring right in your mother's arms
You finally get your blush red kisses at night

Mrs. Banks
by Hayleigh Cook

Mrs. Banks is kind and she's also very neat
She's the best teacher in the world
At least that's what I think

What Does a Cat Know?
by Devyn Pratt

Scratching, licking, purring, kicking
Chasing birds and mice, running all around
Playing, sleeping, meowing, whining
Trotting into town, seeing lots of people
In and out the stores, walk back
Take a nap and hear its kitty snores

Skateboarding
by Avery Steinmetz

Skateboarding is fun, skateboarding is cool
Skateboarding is awesome and you are, too
When you wreck it feels like you break your neck
When you land a trick your stomach feels like you are getting sick
And skateboarding just makes me, me

My Personal Day
by Tyler Capitano

Today's my day, my very special day
Today I sit on my couch and rot away
Today I don't feel like going out to play
Today's my day, my very special day
I need some space from the everyday race
Today's my day, my very special day
Today is my personal day

Yuri Cedeno
by Grace Cedeno

Yuri
Funny and smart
Relative of Grace, Dad
Who likes drawing and working on cars
Who feels God is important
Who would like to see Ecuador once again
Resident of New York
Cedeno

Wonders
by Maddie Green

As I lie awake in bed, I wonder
What are planets like?
How is the Earth round when we are on flat ground?
Why do people die? What is it like to be dead?
What is it like to switch bodies with someone?
What is it like to be a grownup?
As I lie awake in bed, I wonder

Shooting For the Win
by Kathryn Alotta

Fourteen players hold their breath as one takes a shot, shot, shot
The sound of scared fans fill the night sky; will she make it?
Then just like that, the whistle blows
Goal

Dreams
by Nicole Hamer

Everyone has a dream
Whether it is to be a pro baseball player or a famous writer, it is still a dream
You may imagine dreams or the dreams could just happen in life
Some people believe in dreams and some people don't
But dreams will always stay dreams

Inside the Unknown
by Bryan McCartin

Inside the unknown, there isn't anyone, anything, nothing
Nothing happening, dead silence
That's all it is, maybe no one is sure
Many people think that the unknown is just a room
With white walls and nothing in it, just nothing
Some people just think it's space
Space is just a universe of nothing
But I think it's not space, it's just nothing

Dolphin
by Nick Miller

I'm a dolphin as you can see
I love to swim in the sea
My relatives include porpoises and whales
I like to eat squid and fish with scales
I breathe through a hole on the top of my head
I sleep in the water, not in a bed
With one eye open the dolphin can sleep
He sleeps this way to find his prey in the deep

Face
by Jake Martin

Who is that face? What is that face?
Can it be? Is it a she or a he?
It had those eyes like a lonely guy
But it had that hair like a happy little fair
Who is that face? What is that face?
Can it be?
It's my friend, Zoe

How We Changed
by Cameron Kruger

Why is it that the revolting exhaust has to pollute the air?
The Earth has been poisoned with gas; we have changed so much; I am disappointed
The beautiful ducks seem to be the most happiest living thing in the world
The colorful animals laugh with delight, but seem to be moved unpleasantly
By the disgusting fumes; the trees, speaking of old tales
When the mountains stretched to the sky and the meadows long and lush
The water was untouched and sparkling with content
Where skies were beautiful blue, the clouds brought to life
Like fluffy white balls, we have changed too much

Our World
by Evan Dartt

Our world is blue, our world is green
From outer space it can be seen
It is home to you and me
And it is where we are free

The Woman With Long Hair
by Breigh Haase

There once was a woman with long hair
Her favorite food is a pear
She was skinny
And she whinnied
She didn't know what to wear

Matthew
by Matthew Jarvis

Matthew
Nice, knowledgeable, talkative
Wishes to be a great baseball player
Dreams of being a better pitcher than I am now
Wants to play baseball
Who wonders how baseball players are so good at baseball
Who fears getting hit by a pitch
Who is afraid of inaccurate pitchers
Who likes dogs
Who believes the Yankees will win the World Series
Who loves nature
Jarvis

Smiley
by August Harrison

Smiley is a happy smile
Smiley is a thankful smile
Smiley is a promising smile
Smiley doesn't want to die
Smiley plays a lot
Smiley gets friends a lot
Smiley has to smile home now

What Is Blue?
by Rachel Margolin

Blue is the sky
Blue is my eyes
Blue is a pool
This color is so cool
Blue is sadness in the rain
Like having a wound with lots of pain
Blue is a robin's egg laying in a nest
Blue is what is the best!
A bluebird flies across the sky
Flapping his wings as he goes by
The sound of blue is drip... drip ... drip
Like pouring tears
Like a child is crying in fear!
Blue is a lollypop that we suck and suck, and a Jolly Rancher too
No other color can beat this color, and this color is blue
Blue is snow falling in the winter
Blue is a cousin of purple
Blue ...

The Good Days
by Jessica Palmer

I climb high mountains, I jump small trees
I do all this without even skinning my knees
When I wake in the morning, I let nothing in my way
I save the world every single day, but at the end of the day
When my dad kisses me good night
I'm only his super hero, but hey, that's alright
In the day, I wonder if in the next world I'll be the same
But you never know, I might be lame

The Same One
by Claire Volpenhein

I look in the mirror and don't have a clue who it is!
But as I look, it looks like me; but how could it be?
Oh, maybe that person has my hair
But when the next day comes, I look a little better
Now today it has my ears; oh my, it's my dear Aunt Ger

Star
by Bobby Roode

I am a yellow star; you know me for being in a constellation
You know the way I twinkle in the sky and the way I shoot through the sky
My foe is the moon; my friend is the sun
My voice is like bells ringing; my touch is like love
My fear is having no twinkle; my dream is to stay happy
I see Earth below, I hear thunderbolts above me; I feel happy

The Holiday Tree
by Marissa Famiglietti

Mom is the angel on the top of the tree; she's everything good
Dad is the tree at Rockefeller Center; we have to drive to see him
Michael is tangled in lights that make me crazy
I'm the presents wrapped in colorful paper because I am very special

Fireworks
by Ashton Helbert

Fireworks explode in the air
Pretty colors everywhere
People cheering next to me
Now I can't wait till next year

The Cat and the Mat
by Caroline Toomey

There once was a cat
Who liked to sit on a mat
He was so poor
He could not afford a paper door
So he sat and sat on that old, fat mat

What Is Blue?
by Jeremy Dreyer

Blue is ocean water crashing
Blue is feeling sad; you feel blue when you do something bad
Blue is the smell of the ocean wind
The color of a blue jay
I like blue; it's the breeze at the ocean, too!
It's the sound of a violet opening
Color of a really hot fire flame
The son or daughter of purple
Blue is the color on the ground after a snowstorm
Blue is the color of some people's eyes
Blue also is the color of blueberries
Is a color of a sweet and sticky treat that you pull apart
It's the color of M&M's; color of Skittles, too
Blue is cool; do you like blue?

Nadine Nichols
by Shania Nichols

Nadine
Good cook and stylish
Relative of Shania, Mom
Who likes to play solitaire and watch scary movies
Who feels family is very important and everyone should be nice to each other
Who would like to see Denzel Washington
Resident of New York
Nichols

Nature's Presents
by Hannah Melly

When I walk outside, I see the bees buzzing around
All the flowers looking for nectar to snack on
That's nature's present
I see leaves from the maple trees, in my yard, dance in the sparkling sky
That's nature's present
The red, yellow, green, orange, and purple flowers look like a rainbow
Is filling the sky with happiness
That's nature's present
When the sky turns reddish-pink, nature's presents are still watching over you
Bats fly through the sky
Their blackness makes it look as if the sky is moving very fast
So respect nature's presents as if they were yours
If you don't treat nature's presents kindly
You know what will happen ... A storm!

Untitled
by Nick Moir

Talented, hits very far, he can catch
The best I ever saw
Plays the guitar, plays them well
Can you guess who it is?
It is Bernie Williams

White
by Asaf Bhatti

The color of sparkling snow in February
The inside filling of delicious Oreo cookies
The creamy taste of a cold vanilla ice cream
Cool wind blowing in your face
Clouds grumbling through the sky
Bowling balls crashing into pins
A coconut tree getting eaten by a person
Someone drinking cold milk from the fridge
When someone eats marshmallows right after they have melted
Paint that dried like a smooth cloud
Feels like someone pulling your soul out of you
A ray of light shining over you
White makes you think

Morning Sunrise
by Monika Farmer

Beautiful red, orange and pink sunrise coming up from behind the trees
Flickering lights turning on, warm bright sun touching my face
I can taste new morning, damp dew on the grass
Sleepy animals awaking, bird crowing to wake friends
Dogs barking when parents get up, cars starting with adults going to work
Trains coming to carry people to New York City
Morning darkness fades, that's what it's like at morning sunrise

Create Something
by TJ Snape

Create something ... Swift
Create something ... Soft
Create something ... At which I won't have to scoff
Create something ... Cautious
Create something ... Clever
Create something ... I will reject never
Create something ... Weird
Create something ... Wacky
Create something ... Very hack-sacky
Create ... A poem

Thanks For Summer
by Alexis Shinault

Summer is such a delightful season!
It's a present from God; there's no other reason
Playing outside, like I love so much to do
Me, my brothers and all my friends, too!
The smell of BBQ all through the air
School's out and there's not a care
So when I lay down to say my prayers at night
I thank God for such a wonderful sight

Spring
by Bria Agard

Spring is fun and playtime
It's time to rise and shine
Take a dip in the pool
It's really, really fun
Everywhere you look you see spring all around
Spring is fun and playtime
It's time to rise and shine

What Is Blue?
by Erin Hunt

Nice is blue and beautiful; some mice are blue
Blue is the ocean on a nice day with the feeling of delight on everyday
It is a feeling of excitement on a sunny day
Blue is more popular than you think ... it is a dad to green
A little bit of winter and a little bit of summer waves
Blue are the waves on a beautiful day

Four Seasons
by Hannah Hobby

Four seasons are here
Subtract three, and winter is near
Frostbite is around the corner
After winter comes spring with light jackets, and it rains no doubt
That's what spring is all about!
Add two more seasons, then summer is here
And t-shirts are final and clear
One multiplied by four gives all the seasons
Now I have given you all the winter, spring, summer, and autumn reasons!

My Busy Dizzy Family!
by Jeslin Malayil

My mom is sleeping, my dad is snoring
My brother is dizzy; I don't know why he is always turning around!
My sister is busy reading a book; everyone calls her book worm
And she doesn't even know what a book worm is!
That is why I call them a busy dizzy family!

My Guardian Angel
by Gabrielle Sokira

My guardian angel I never met
I wish I could just catch him in a net
He is always protecting me
Even while watching the sea
I wish I could just hear him once
While we both eat lunch
He is a bird
That I've always heard
I wish I could see him
Then I would win

The Silly Soccer Kids
by Jessica Schulman

The goalie is singing
The coach is sleeping
The defense is picking his nose
The offense is sucking his toes
That's why the team let the ball go
No wonder the day is going real slow

The Bunny
by Kate Hahn

I saw a little bunny and I thought it was cute
And it can play the flute!
But it wasn't really that funny
So, I gave it some money
But it had been down the garbage shute
When we were watching TV, he pushed "mute"
And it loved to eat honey; it didn't have a sock
It didn't have a date
And it didn't go to school
It didn't know how to mock
It didn't have a mate
But I can say one thing and it was very cool

Happiness Is Yellow
by Julianna Russo Friedman

Happiness is yellow
It sounds like the wind blowing
It smells like a chocolate mousse cake
It tastes like a lemon meringue pie
It looks like a butterfly fluttering its wings
Happiness feels like the warm sun heating you

I Am
by Julia Hyacinthe

I am a great friend that adores horses
I wonder if there is a shining gold horse flying in the air
With my name on its saddle pad
I hear stallions galloping on the field beneath me
I see the world as I ride on my gorgeous horse
I want to have a horse of my own to cherish and take care of forever
I am a great friend that adores horses
I pretend to be a horse trainer
I feel the silky, scaly wings of my majestic horse
I touch the soft, puffy clouds as my head goes through them
I worry if my horse will die and I will fall off
I cry when mine and all horses die
I am a great friend who adores horses
I understand that when I get old I won't be able to ride
I say all horses should be free, but able to be ridden
I dream about the day I get a horse of my own
I try to ride my best whenever I can
I hope to ride forever and ever
I am a great friend that adores horses

Unicorns
by Sara Coto

Pretty as a picture
Mane soft like a pillow
Nose wet as a river and cold like winter
Wisping softly through the night
As if they weren't there
Pretty unicorns

Dear Lord
by Sara Neuman

Dear Lord, thank You for what You have done
Dear Lord, I am happy You sent Your only Son
Dear Lord, please help me to do what is always right
And keep me safe all through the night
And all through the day when the sun is out
When I am to be quiet, don't let me make a riot
In school, please help me to listen to my studies
Dear Lord, thank You for loving me

True Blue Friend
by Morgan Travis

Always be there for you, even when you're acting cuckoo
Lifts you up when you're down and keeps you from acting like a clown
Never leaves your side, even when you want to hide
Plays with you when you need someone and reminds you to always have fun
Be with you to the end and always wants to be your friend

Horse
by Britt Hanson

A horse lies high up in the hills
Smelling the spring flowers and the fresh air
He stops, spots and gallops towards me
Down, down, down the hill he runs
He stops at my feet, then stares into my eyes
Just like he wants to tell me something
I get on and away we ride
Into the sun setting above meadows
Of freshly bloomed spring flowers

Wildlife
by Katie Hamlin

Simple and silent, cautious and creepy
Mysterious and mystic, brown and green, peaceful and pleasant
Take a walk on the wild side, it could change you forever
You begin to understand the big and little
You find your inner peace, soothing and secret, calm and quiet
The animals, the birds, the feelings that overtake you
The piney smell, the mountainous view, the dirt carpet, the cloudy blanket
The covered-canvas of color, feelings, smell smells ... wildlife

My Dad
by Cody Hufnagel

I love my dad
Even when he makes me mad
We play a lot of ball
Not only in the fall
My dad, so happy and mad

Frogs on Ice
by Ashley Taul

Frogs on ice
One had lice
And didn't want to give it to the other
So he decided they wouldn't be friends with one another!

Dragons
by Todd Stuckman

Dragons green, red, brown or blue
They don't scare me but do they scare you?
Scorching, smoldering, vicious bite
Furious dragons are not a delight

About the Author
by Anthony Lacy

Anthony Lacy
3rd grader in elementary school
He lives in Oregon with his grandma and grandpa, 2 sisters and 2 brothers
His favorite thing to do is play video games

What Is Orange
by Travis Gozley

Orange flows out of a fireplace, blazing very hot in the winter
You see a blue dot but if no fire is built, you will grow cold
What else is orange? A math book is orange, foxes are too
Did you hear? The two colors that make orange are red and yellow too
They are also relatives
Orange is like a beautiful summer day, when the sun begins to fade away
Orange is in the fall, when the leaves fall from the bare trees
The sound of fluttering leaves
Orange smells like an orchard of oranges, on vacation in Florida
But the best thing is the feeling of orange!
It's a mild color, not angry, not sad, but orange is not mad

What Love Can Do To You
by Sofia Ponce

I like this boy who was full of disaster
But my crush on him grew faster and faster
My friends encouraged me to ask him out
But he brought disappointment to my face and made me shout
I expressed my feelings and told him how I really felt
His explanation to my question really made me melt
I discovered he really did like me and he was shy
I can tell by the way he looked at me and didn't budge or blink an eye
At first I was confused on how our relationship would emerge
After kissing him a little I just couldn't stop the urge
He was a convenient boyfriend and was always agreeable and sweet
His ability to show affection was always very discrete
I deserved to be treated like a princess with enthusiasm and love
His curiosity was amazing, it was like he was sent from above

Butterflies
by Vanessa Silvestri

Butterflies
Colorful, flat wings
Their wings collide in the sky
They flutter around

Auntie
by Khadijah Harden

My auntie loved to laugh and have fun
She always made people feel good; people adored her
Every time she walked into a room, the room would fill up with happiness
She always gave people hugs and kisses; my family really loved her
Her friends, people at her job and people at home all loved her
Now that she's gone, all the fun is gone
I know that she's where she belongs; she can have fun in Heaven, too
Our family wishes that she was still here with us
I will always remember that her favorite game was charades
Now that's my favorite game
I know in my heart that we will always love her
I miss her a lot and I can't get her off my mind; I love her a lot

What Is Red?
by Thomas DaCosta

Red is the sound of someone's temper
Red is a tomato, a chili, a pepper, a nice little flower
Red is a rose, watering it with a hose
Red is a feeling of your anger; you'll just want to throw a big red hanger
Red is very hot in the Earth's core; they're like waves crashing on the ocean's shore
Red is very smart; just like your brain as though it works just like a train
Red is the summer; the weather will be hot, you will burn up and feel like a dot
After one day of school, pink went to bed and her mother said her sister was red

My Girl
by Katherine Elizabeth Wilson

You won't find my girl at the mall
You will find her at the pet store
You won't find my girl at any Little Miss Contest
You will find her at a pet show
You won't find my girl at the bakery
You will find her at the barkery
You won't find my girl at the dinner table
You will find her under the table stealing my meat
For my girl is a dog named Sadie

Friendship
by Amanda Jones

I know a girl, we are best friends forever
Which means we will always stick together
There's also another girl that I know
But sometimes I wonder if she's my friend or foe
Friends are who should always trust each other
Even if I dislike her brother
Friends are awesome, friends are nice
Just hope they never get head lice
We share our toys and talk about boys
I wonder what I would do if she ever moved

Summer Ends
by Madeline Amzler

Summer fades as fall comes to replace it
Fireflies blink off their yellow lights as the sun falls to the ground
Burned golden leaves drop onto piles
Splashes from pools grow quiet
Mosquitoes buzzes sleep, leaves crackling like maracas
Healing of the stinging sunburn goes away
Moist colorful leaves stick to kids' dry palms
Juicy watermelon sweetens kids' taste-buds
Sugary candy drops into throats
Smoky scent from people's backyards come forward
Pumpkin pie sweetens houses from the oven
Summer is in pajamas while fall is in clothes

Puppy, Puppy
by Tawnie Johnson

Puppy, puppy
Jump and play
You are so cute
You are so fun
You are a big ball of fun to me and she
We love you so, so much
I think it is puppy love

Coaster Thrills
by Samantha Millmann

Waiting in line, my heart beats fast
Anxious, nervous, palms all sweaty
In my seat, the ride starts with a jolt
Pitch black, sharp turns
Loop-de-loops, hands waving
Screaming with all my might!
Stumbling off the ride, still dizzy
Heart racing with excitement
I find myself running, not away
But to get back on the end of the line
- Dedicated to my mom, dad and sister Nicole
for going on a wonderful trip to Disney World and exploring lots of coasters!

Tulips
by Jacquelyn Sullivan

Soft, smooth, velvety
Staying as straight as a tree
Growing to the sky

Lime Green
by Jamie Mosbrucker

My sheets on my bed; my favorite Sunriver hoodie
Numbers on a digital clock; an artist painting a picture
A baby frog croaking; chewing Laffy Taffy
A fresh just grown lime; a pixie full of sugar
Yummy lime Gatorade after a day's hard work
The warmth of the sun; spring just beginning
The queezy feeling in my stomach; lime green makes me relax

Life
by Aster Samuel

Lightly as the wind
As down to earth as the green grass
As angry as a waterfall
As confusing as the past
But that's the way life goes
Yes, that's the way life goes

Today's the Day
by Chrishan Fernando

Today's the day of fun and games
Today's the day to jump and play
Today's the day birds are chirping
Today's the day the river runs free
There is no foe or enemy; there's naught but friends and family
You see it's clear; there's nothing to fear
'Tis a perfect day; you know it's true!
So get off that seat; be on your way
Don't be sour; if you're nice you'll have power
Not the power to control, not the power to bowl
But the power to befriend and yes, the power to play on this wonderful day

A Magnet On a Wall
by Zolvany Nunez

The morning ... a magnet on a wall, so happy in the day
Teachers use me to hold up important things
Children love to laugh with me when I drop papers to the floor
Teachers don't like that which I don't adore
During lunch I love to watch everybody doing child things
After lunch ... lunch is over, kids are working on work that has to be done
Teachers answer the phone; so bored on the wall, nothing to do
Friends and I planning on the party
Still so bored, friends asleep, kids packing up
The night ... a magnet so lonely and sad at night
Friends awake, making snacks, party is about to start and more of us coming in
My friend's trying to make me happy, Maggie said, "Have some fun"
I had to agree, she's my friend
At the party ... Maggie was right about having fun
Talking to friends, playing party games, eating chocolate covered strawberries
I'll see the children tomorrow from the wall, no papers to hold, just fun
After party ... time to clean up, party is over
Everything has to be spotless or the teacher would be unhappy
Time to go to bed, for I have to go to work in the morning
For a magnet on the wall I am

Invisible Friend
by Danielle Kramer

As I lay happily in the crystal clean snow
The wind sneaks behind me and bites my cheek
He speaks of all the great wonders he has seen
He has traveled slowly through the fifty states and over hot dry continents
He inquires if I can take some time to play with him
His coldness surrounds me and I want to play in his wintry wonderland
Sadly I hear a call coming from my home
I make my way over the icy ground with my friend pushed at my back
I take one last look at my invisible friend but he is not there
He has gone on to travel once more

Watching Grass
by Maximilian Crean

Watching the green grass
Swaying, reaching for the sky
Watching it grow high

My Cat Muffin
by Lily Cuyler

My mom thinks she is funny, my dad thinks she is fat
Sometimes I call her 'Bunny', because she runs like that
She thinks she is the princess, and must have milk served on a platter
It leaves her with a mess, but little does she know, it will only make her fatter
She walks along quite slow, her hunting is quite poor
So she relies upon her brother to bring her more and more
Mostly she is lazy; mostly she is slow
How much it is I love her, only she will ever know
I guess right now I'll tell you who this poem's for
My darling little kitty, I love you forever more!

Murphy
by Rose Raza

Aunt Nancy's dog
Fluffy, fuzzy, playful
Jumping all day
Murphy
A little annoying
But loveable

Dimitri Jones
by Isaiah Jones

Dimitri
Rough and fun
Relative of Isaiah, cousin
Who likes to play football
Who feels tough and bad
Who would like to see New Jersey
Resident of New York
Jones

Popcorn
by Vinny Biordi

As crunchy as pretzels
As creamy as ice cream
Smells so tasty! Could already smell it
Could hear popping noise!
That's popcorn

The Tropical Rainforest
by Kyle Bannon

There is a wonderful river with animals around it drinking
And fish splashing in the river
There are many tropical flowers surrounding it
I see a big rock, so I sit on it and look around
I see the wonderful, blue sky and the amazing animals
They make many sounds ... a monkey howling, dry leaves crackling, snakes hissing
The sun is rising; when it comes up, it is colorful
I wonder where exactly I am in this amazing, tropical rainforest ...

Yellow
by Kyeanna Henry

A happy little smiley face, a cozy sweater
The stroke of a highlighter, a little girl guzzling her lemonade
The buzzing of a bumblebee, a big school bus
A sour lemon, sweet and sticky honey
A bitter sweet banana, warmth like a blanket
Powerful like lightning, soft like a chick's feathers
Yellow can make you happy

Caramel Apples
by Phill Coreas

Caramel apples are delicious
Juicy, tasty, yummy
Sweet, sticky, gooey
Candied, brown, crunchy
But not sour

Deer
by Jordan Crawford

Deer
Scared, hiding
Fighting, eating, hunted
Losing antlers, scraping trees
Deer

Dragon Flight
by Andrew Marine

There they go ... over the mountain to be with their family
After seeing them, I feel so great in the sun
Dragons fly so very high in the sky
A big cloud over them, and the dragons vanish

Springtime
by Ryan Meller

When it is springtime the flowers grow back again
The air is warm; the leaves grow back on trees
Children play outside; children play in the park
The sun rises earlier; the sun sets later
People ride bikes and people play sports
Spring is a nice season

Blue
by Shianne Mammon

Blue is the color of the rain, sea and water
Blue is the color that everyone wears; like shirts, jeans and shoes
Blue is the color that matches your eyes
Do you like the color blue?

Twilight
by Hannah Gill

The hazy blues desperately grasp each other
Trying to keep the night away
But the strong shoulders of night push away the twilight
And sends a burly hand clasping the earth
As he climbs to the top and claims the sky for his own

Snowflakes
by Catherine Tignetti

Breezy bits of bitter icy cold ice, blow in wind
Its edges shine so brightly
The pictures on it are beyond your wildest dreams
They are all different from each other in every way that it seems
Just like I said before
But now everything on it is now bright too, just like me and you
When you look out the window in the morning
After it has been falling for a couple of hours
It looks like big piles of white fluffy marshmallows on the ground
What am I? Snowflakes!

Flowers
by Lucy Rodriguez

Pluck me a flower so beautiful and bright
Pluck me a flower for I will have much delight
Is it a rose, a violet or a daisy?
Pluck me a flower so beautiful and bright

Sports
by Greer Neff

Sports, sports, there are so many to choose from
But I, Greer, only like some
Basketball and soccer are right for me
When I'm practicing my sports, let me be
You better watch out, here I come

Me, Myself, and I
by Meagan McGinnis

My hair is like a beautiful, long blonde bale of hay
My eyes are like round, brown mud puddles
With somebody's black shoe stepping into them
My feet are like small flowers with five petals on them
My brain is a big blob of thoughts rolling around inside my head
My heart holds an empty feeling and passion
That is broken as much as a crack in the cement
I am an iPod and eat music

Fishing
by Ashley Krantz

You were fishing in the water when the boat went teeter, totter
Put the bait on the hook and the rod tip shook
You look at the hook and the bait was still there
You were too late and the fish already left
That's a pity, it was a big one too; the lure is going crazy!
You caught one! Uncle Lue only bought one, he's a cheater!

Beach
by Nicole Laghezza

Peaceful, joyful, relaxing, ocean water crashing against the rocks
Colorful bathing suits, aqua-blue water, hyper kids playing and laughing
The imprint of a seagull's foot stands before me
The white lifeguard chair stands out like a diamond in a dark cave
The shadow of the big umbrellas protect people's feet from the hot sand
Brightly covered towels cover the beach
And as I sit, I wonder ...
How many shells are at the bottom of this big ocean?

Cottage Cheese
by Justus Newell

Cottage cheese, I don't like
I'll run over it with a motorbike

The Ninja
by Connor Hallett

Shuriken in air
Calling card of the Ninja
The ground soon stained red

Green
by Pedro Juarez

The leaves on a mighty tree
A big bowl of jiggly Jell-o
The green grass outside
Fallen leaves crunching
A cricket chirping
A frog croaking
A sour grape
A ripe kiwi
An apple, green and sweet
A warm sweater
A crayon that my brother threw at me
The grass when I fall
Green makes you happy

Car
by Tiffany Fuschetto

Car
Fast, hard
Driving, pushing, bumping
Fun to drive it
Vehicle

Guidance
by Kalli Albertus

Adults don't have all the answers, neither do the children
But the children do look up at someone in their life
To give them guidance and wise thoughts
But sometimes the children do the same thing to adults
So the adults can listen and see what they've taught their young child

Global Warming
by Jason Klein

Smokestacks steaming, trash on the streets
The sun is gleaming, while the Earth heats
Ice caps melt, shores overflow
We all felt heating is a no
Nothing done, we're having no fun
While the South Pole melts, our progress is none
Something must be done soon, we must start before noon
Because if nothing is completed, the Earth will be way too heated

My Red Trans Am
by Tanner Wathen

My Trans Am doesn't run
Fixing it up will be fun
I need to wash it
Because it's dusty
I need to paint it
Because it's rusty!

A Fly
by Brian Toman

A homeless person's like a fly who's always being swatted
No one wants to look at your face and you feel out of place
But when that charity comes 'round, every one sees how bad they've been
And they see you're no different than you or me

Tornado
by Melissa Martire

I am a tornado
You know me for the storm that comes in hot places
You know the way I twist and turn
And the way I hurt people badly
My foe is the weatherman
My friend is hot and cold air
My voice is like the roar of a lion
My touch is like a powerful bee sting
My fear is the sun
My dream is to damage the world
I see people hiding
I hear screaming
I feel pointy nails from houses

Sick
by Diann Miller

I cannot go to school today
Said little Diann Marie McKay
I have the yucky chicken pox
My head feels like it's full of rocks
My nose is wet, my skin is red
That's why I'm laying in my bed
Maybe I've got the whooping cough
My hair feels like it's falling off
My left hand is turning green
There's the biggest wart I've ever seen
What's that? What's that you say?
You say today is ... Saturday?
Goodbye, I'm going out to play

Snow
by Samantha Incalcaterra

Snow, a white blanket over the earth
As soft as a pillow, as white as a sheep
As light as a feather, like little white balls
Drifting in the wind, covering the trees
Covering the rooftops of every little house

Middle School
by Samantha Sobieski

Middle school is hard; middle school is tough
And I just have to say, "I've had enough!"
We have a test; I flunked just like the rest; we got skunked!
We have to read; I'm so bad; I don't succeed; it's really sad
So here I am on the couch; I quit school like a slouch
I went back; I guess it's okay; I had to pack; I'm on my way!
Now I'm there ... Some A's! No more being scared, hooray!

Easter
by Elise Easton

Easter egg hunts all around
Colorful eggs on the ground
When the Easter bunny comes door to door
No one knows what he has in store
Gifts, happiness, and cheerfulness in the air
Cute bows in little girls' hair
Let's hope today it does not rain
The happiness Easter brings we cannot explain
In our baskets are lots of candies
Maybe a gift card to a store called Mandee's
It is time to have some fun
Let's go play out in the sun
We've all been waiting for this day
Happy Easter! It's today!

Nighttime
by Kaleigh Feldkamp

The sun sets; the flowers close; dark settles upon the earth
The oceans still; the owls hoot; the birds nest
The moths come out; the stars rise; the moon is full
The night is clear; everything is still

What Is Blue?
by Adam Napolitano

Blue is the beautiful sky of the morning start
Blue is the color of your clothes when you get dressed in the morning
Blue is the beautiful ocean when you hear the sounds of the waves
Blue is the sad feeling if I don't win the shopping spree
Blue is the color of ice pops when you take that delicious bite
Blue is the color of blue jays, which means spring is here
Blue is the screen of your computer when you log into a game
And blue is the color of your pen when you write on that piece of paper

Great Oak
by Allison Biancardi

I am the Great Oak, tall and enormous
Making shade and resources before us
Giving oxygen to mankind below
Standing up to the sun, watching it glow
I am the jungle gym, open arms for mankind
Playing hide and seek, children run, play and hide
I am the shield blocking predators from prey
In my acorn-covered leaves, they hide away
I am the Great Oak, tall and enormous
Making shade and resources before us

It All Began
by Tyler Moon

It all began with a speck of dust
Then it began to gather different things like metal and plastic, even a big glass door
Suddenly it began to blacken and its size changed very fast, as well as its color
Then its mouth opened and it said the most soothing things
The voice is something you must hear, for it made everyone burst
But not into balls of goo or flames burning everything
But into laughter from you and me; everyone liked, then loved it, too
For it made little notes of blue when it used that mellow voice
To cheer up me and you

Nature's Math
by Raleigh Brown

Summer, autumn, winter, spring ... which one is best?
Summer with bright flowers, beautiful flowers
And when it gets hot, add some yummy popsicles!
Autumn has crunchy leaves; subtract some warmth but keep some, too
Rake the leaves, catapult into them, fun, fun, fun!
Winter, you multiply snow and icicles, make a snowman
Then jump into a warm blanket inside; drink all the hot cocoa with family!
Spring, divide the warmth and the cold, flowers start to bud, subtract lots of snow!

Trees Are Like Bees
by Autumn Brumley

Trees are like bees
Neither eats peas
Because they're allergic to Febreeze
They sit around and sneeze
Trees and bees don't need keys
They definitely don't eat cheese
But only trees surely can freeze!

School
by Madelyn Strycker

My name is Madelyn Mae and I'm here to say
My teacher, Mrs. V, drinks a lot of tea
I especially love math; it sends me on the right path
Recess is even better; you don't have to write one letter
Then there's lunch; today we're having brunch
Then we have a reading test, so it's time to do my best
Then we have science, which is so much fun
We get to do experiments out in the sun!
At the end of the year, you'll hear us cheer
But some will pout 'cause school is out!

Whale
by Noah Davis

The young whale would play all day
He had great hearing so he never asked, "What did you say?"
He had a favorite dish
That was fish
Even though he's grown up and mature
He'll never be able to grow any fur

Beach Rise
by Lexis Arielle Tudisco

Seagulls swoop down to the crystal clear saltwater to catch dinner
Crashing white waves rise high, fall, kissing the sand
Sipping the salty water, gagging
Swimming underwater against the gold sand, kicking my legs, stroking my arms
A colorful sunrise appearing among the light blue ocean
Purple, yellow, orange and blue fill the sky
Slowly trotting on the moist sand leaving footprints behind
Disappearing in the darkness

Silent Snow
by Tara Korkus

Peering through the window, crystal snow falls
Silence gives my ears calmness
Cold outside, warm inside
Sitting on cozy bed, icicles hanging from roof top
Snow spilling from the sky
Piles of snow covers ground
White snow, silence!

The Four Seasons
by Maggie Keisler

Winter
Multiply the cold, subtract the heat
And add a little marshmallow, then divide the sweets
Spring
Divide the snow, add the flowers
Subtract all the ice, then multiply the rain
Summer
Multiply the pools, subtract the tornadoes, add the lemonade
Autumn
Multiply the leaves, subtract the pools, add the pumpkin pie

What Is Yellow?
by Erika Swenson

Yellow feels nice and warm
When the sun comes up after a storm
Yellow is as bright as the sun
When the sun comes out and the moon is done
Yellow is the smell of a rose
That gives you a tingle in your nose
Yellow is the color of lightning
That can always give me a frightening

4-H Show Day
by Taylor Fisher

Wake up on 4-H Show day; so excited at first
Then heart dropping; so nervous once inside the show ring
What if he jumps? What if he runs away?
You can't turn back now!
Judge comes over; questions, suggestions
My cheeks feel hot with worry
Sweat running down my face like a river
Unnecessary fear ... second place!

Spring
by Amber Schmidt

It was a spring day
When I went out to play
I love the sun
And soon I was having fun
But it was during May

Call Out To Jesus
by Nathan Allen

When it seems everyone is against you and are rooting for you to fail
It is the name of the Lord, Jesus Christ, upon which you should hail
For He will love and care for you, for He, Himself, is love
The Chosen One, Messiah, Heaven's Perfect Dove
So in times when it seems everyone is against you and are rooting for you to fail
Just believe and God will hear your hail

War
by Madison Murphy

The ground is bloody; the sound of a gun
This is war and it's not fun
So many lives are spared a night
In an awful, noisy fight
Thoughts of battle in a mind
Soldiers want to leave them all behind
In a battle, many die
Some yell, some cry
They cannot wait to go home to their families
To lie in the sun, under the trees
Still, thoughts linger like an echo in a cave
Our soldiers who left were strong and brave

Why, Where, When, Who, and How
by Eric Birnbaum

Why did they invent why?
Where did they create where?
When did they create when?
Who wrote the word who?
How did they think of why, where, when, who and how?

Mother Nature
by Dallas Prusi

A beautiful glimmer above the waterfall catches my eye
I look to the animals; they look back
They look confused, as if I'm here to hurt them, but I came to comfort them
Tall trees are tired; they sway to the water as it crashes down against rocks
What is Mother Nature thinking?
I look to the sun; it's light pink in color
My shadow shows what I am doing, standing on the strong branches of a tall tree
The bees are in a hurry, as if their season is almost gone
What is Mother Nature thinking? Nobody knows for sure ...

My Self-Portrait
by Daniel Nguyen

My hair is like an ever-changing foliage of a forest
My eyes are brown like fresh soil
My brain is a huge calculator
My heart holds hatred as strong as cinder blocks
I live in a video game and eat batteries

Puggsley
by Shadna Kime

Puggsley
Cute, soft
Cuddly, playful, big
Breaks things, wrinkly
Barks like a seal
Curled lip, funky
Dog

What Is Yellow?
by Samantha Sturken

Yellow is awesome, yellow is bold
Yellow is like the second daughter of gold
Yellow is bright and gives off light
A field of daisies is a beautiful sight
Yellow is caution; it means slow down
But it's a great color for banners all around town
Yellow is happy, not really sad
It's mostly good, not usually bad
Yellow is cake and this is true
This poem's not a fake and I hope neither are you
Yellow is summer, which for most people isn't a bummer
Unless you have to study, then I normally hook up with a buddy
Yellow is bang! Yellow is boom!
These you can hear in a quiet room
Yellow is scattered more than here and there
Look out your window, I'm sure you'll find it there!

The Earth
by Tyson Crawford

The grass is green
The water is blue
The clouds are white
And the lakes are green

Cosby Is a Funny Dog
by Hannah Johnson

Cosby is a funny dog
Cosby can be such a hog!
Cosby likes to swim, swim, swim
I like to play with him, him, him
Cosby likes to ride on a golf cart
So sad we can't take him to Wal-Mart!
Cosby is a special pup
He can fetch, shake, and sit up
Cosby likes to chase cars
Too bad he can't walk on Mars

The Moon
by Brayden Michael

The moonlight shines down out of the midnight sky
For he is very sly, he watches me as I lay
As if he were an invisible guardian, he protects me from the darkness
As he protects me, being as brave as he can be
He soon grows with despair, for I am paying no attention to him

A Light In Me
by Alex Huber

There is a light in me, there truly is
That makes me happy everywhere
I hate to be sad; I hate to be mad
And there truly is a light in me

What a Vulture Needs to Know
by J.J. McNown

Dead mammals, big birds hovering in a circle
Dead trees waiting, eating, watching
Kidneys, lower intestine, blood, war, fights, heights
House is a rib cage, eyeballs are appetizers
The feeling of carcass squeezing through their cheeks as they swallow it
The screeches of puppies, kitties, elephants
Baby cows, baby mammals, baby dogs, and baby camels
And unstringing the lines on your brain

Monkeys
by Caitlin Reusch

Monkeys are so fluffy
As fluffy as can be
It makes you want to sleep on them
So why don't you try and see

What Is Gold?
by PJ DeVito

My favorite color is gold
Gold is the color of the leaves in the fall
Gold is the color of a shiny ball
Gold is a cool color
Gold is hard like a rock
You can count it on a dock
You can put gold in your mouth
When I touch it, I feel happy
When I hear bling-bling or caching-caching, I think of gold
I feel relaxed when I touch gold
I feel like going in a pool of gold
Or getting a gold jewel
I have a tool that is gold but it has mold
A relative to gold is silver
I know a pig named Wilber
Wilber has a gold coat
But then he fell into a moat
Gold is the color of hair
Gold is not the color of a bear
Gold is at the end of the rainbow
When I touch gold I say, "Wow"
Gold is my favorite color

Soccer Sorrow
by David Calvache

You feel the adrenaline rush when the referee blows the whistle
When the ball is in play you try your best to get the ball
When you do you go for a breakaway, but the ball is stolen from you
And all of a sudden the other team scores a goal
You feel the worst out of your whole team
Because you know it started when they stole the ball from you
When the game is over knowing you lost
You go back to your house and you are filled with sorrow

Till Death Did His Part
by Alexis Morris

There once was a small dalmatian who lived in the old fire station
They called him Billy; he loved their chili and never went on vacation
The nights and mornings he worked, rushed by and by
Yet his work was never done, not until he would die
It was sad when that night came; everything was the same ...
Until he slipped and fell into flames
Disappearing into ashes; he has a gravestone now, tall and engraved with sorrow
But his soul will live on past today and tomorrow

Fall
by Renee Rant

Fall
Leaves orange
Leaves fall everywhere
Everyone jumping in leaves
Autumn

I Am
by Erica Bowman

I am an extraordinary girl who loves animals
I wonder if all animals could fly
I hear the wild roars of the forest
I see the animals beneath me
I want to ride free with the ocean animals
I am an extraordinary girl who loves animals
I pretend to soar with the mountains
I feel like one with nature
I touch a dog-shaped cloud in the sly
I worry about losing a furry friend
I cry when a family member is lost forever
I am an extraordinary girl who loves animals
I understand I will never have a pet with fur
I say everything has a mystery behind it
I dream of soaring with the dolphins
I try to be a vet doctor when I grow up
I hope to have a pet someday
I am an extraordinary girl who loves animals

Oh No!
by Deborah Campozano

Oh, no!
My dog ate my homework
And I'm late for school
I lost my backpack
Along with my school stuff
Oh, no!
I have to stay indoors during recess!
Oh, no!

Bite By Bite
by Jordan Ferry

An apple, so round and perfect, will always be consumed
Bite by bite, the apple changes; one fourth, one half, until all that is left is the core
But you can always get another apple to eat all over again
One day ends out so perfect; the next, your life has changed
So frustrated and disappointed, angry, mad and just want to cry
At last, you want to explode, but you always have another day to live all over again

Sugar Is the Sweetest
by Christa Parkes

Roses are red, violets are blue, sugar is sweet and you can be, too
Smell a flower then sing a song, the song can be anything
Long or short, it won't matter
Make it up or sing one you know; maybe write one poem or so
Have fun with what you write; just go with the flow or go talk to Jo Jo
Maybe make it about a cat or kitten, and maybe a dog and a mitten
When you write your dreams on paper there, they will always come true
Even if they don't, it's always a lesson to learn; you always have education
Sugar is the sweetest, babies are cute and sweet
You'd like to be like it forever, but we can't
But we will live forever with love in every part of our body

Softball Games
by Corinne Figoski

A person is up to bat
And she's right on the mat
The ball was already hit
As it comes right to my mitt
The crowd cheers with so much excitement
The team is full of delightment
I throw the ball to home plate
"She's out, that number 8"
"Wow! This is great!"
We win!

When I Say, "I Do"
by Allison Gross

The sound of your voice is soft
I listen from a loft
The sound of your voice makes me smile
Even from the farthest mile
Even though we might not ever be
I would like to wait and see
I saved this poem for you
For the day I say, "I do"

Nature
by Alexandra Louigarde

Mother Nature is surrounding us; the sunsets, the flowers bloom
It feels like we are already in June
The grass is greener than it was before, romances beginning, birds singing
The seas are bluer and new life is knocking
Come with me and see the better side of life
The sunsets, flowers blooming, greener grass
Singing birds and bluer seas; to see all the wonderful things I see
Take my hand and follow me
The signs are very clear, so don't be left out
Because summer is around for only 3 months

Birds of the Sky
by Emory Klopfenstein

The first of the sky, I see it, here comes a V
One leading all the rest from the south
They bring us feathers to find
The nests they nurture till time has come
They go and come in a V
Birds of the sky
Come from the south to watch us, us to watch them
Here for the sun's warmth till it leaves again, just like them
Never know what they are saying
"Will the wind blow, or just my luck?"
Birds of the sky

Waterfall Crashing
by Katherine Foley

Waterfall crashing
Fluffy clouds floating by
Birds chirping
Wind rustling
Bunny hopping along
Bright, yellow sun shining
Leaves rustling through the wind
Waterfall crashing
Lilly pads floating
Squirrels nibbling acorns
Waterfall crashing

Grandma's Cookies
by Logan Thompson

Grandma liked cookies so much
It was a nice day, such a good day for cookies to bake
Grandma loves heart-shaped cookies to make
The cookies taste delicious; I smell something scrumptious
Some try to buy one for a dime; I find the icing like slime
My cookie color is red; they take me to a soft bed
They stick in my stomach like glue; I'm sleeping all the night through

Morning
by Tatiana E. Ferraro

Blue birds chirp and sing
All the church bells ring
A chorus of yawns
At the sound of dawn
Wake up and smell the fresh air
The day is pleasant and fair
Go run along and play
It is a wonderful day
Sing aloud
While the good-natured crowd
Is cheering for you today

What Is Yellow?
by Emily Nosworthy

Yellow is the morning sun
Dandelions blooming on the run
Yellow is a happy, smiley face
The feathers of a canary
The sweet juice from a pineapple
The summer squash from the garden
A yoke of an egg cooking in a pan
A scale of a goldfish, flickering in the water
When you see yellow, you need to slow down!
Yellow is a happy color when you are down
Yellow is the sound of birds chirping all around
Gold is the mother of a fun, yellow color
Yellow is Gatorade when you are sweaty and hot
Yellow is the season of summer
Yellow is the daughter of gold, and the niece of orange
Yellow is the best color of all!

Jesus
by Kassandra M. Locke

Jesus risked His life
He loved us with all His heart
He lives in Heaven

Secrets About Me
by Rachel MacDougall

I am as quiet as a mouse scurrying across the floor
I am as fast as a greyhound running a race
I am as hungry as a bear waking up from a long hibernation
I am as shy as a quail being chased by a hunting beagle
I am as smart as a blue dolphin splashing through the icy water
I am as strong as a husky pulling a heavy sled
I am as sly as a fox stalking its prey
I am as playful as a kitten chasing a tangled ball of yarn
I am as happy as a chocolate Lab running into the refreshing blue ocean
I am Rachel

The Famous Dog
by Megan Rainey

There once was a famous dog
Who found a bone the size of a log
His name was Sparky
He was not barky
He worked as a scientist
Rather than a meteorologist

Blue
by Melina Hunt

Blue is the swaying ocean, going back and forth
It is a bright balloon that is floating in the air
A blue jay's feather falling from the sky
The large eagle singing for a mate
A small baby crying for help
A never-ending soft lullaby
My grandma's homemade cookies, hot off the stove
Sweet venison, right off the grill
Homemade cupcakes that I made myself
My fingers squishing my pillow
The soft, silky fur of my cat
Rubbing my finger on the petal of a rose
Blue can take you to another world

Bluebird
by John Peter Napolitano

Big, blue feathers shine
Bright, yellow beak, hard and smooth
Soaring from the south

What Is Red?
by Ashley Keane

Red is like a fire
Red is heat running through a wire
Red is a feeling of love and passion
Red is a pretty, fall fashion
Red is a cherry on an ice cream sundae
Red is a pile of leaves on a cool, breezy day
Red is a hot, summer day bathing in a pool all day
Red is a rose and a clown's nose
Red is a cardinal flying around a nest
Red is the best!
Red is the sound of a fire truck's siren, "Wee, woo, wee, woo!"
Red is the cousin of orange
Red ...

Night To Day
by Erin-Ashley Ricks

Colors fading, darkness invading, night engulfs the day
Moon light, star bright, night will not stay
Golden splendor, dark offender, the sun brings the day

Little Caterpillar
by Katie Hicks

Little, gray caterpillar sits on a branch
Sadly watching birds circle above him
He knows his death awaits
He thinks of his family and friends for the last time
Then ... Shriek! Swoop! Gone forever

Baby Brother
by Ashlee Quinones

My baby brother, he is so cute
He dances, he sings, he walks, he runs, he talks
My baby brother is the cutest baby on Earth

Giant Squid
by Tyler Strunk

The squid is a giant creature
I wouldn't want it as my teacher
The giant squid is a carnivore
It would be scary to see it at your front door
The giant squid's eyes are as big as beach balls
It can grow up to be thirty-three feet tall
The giant squid lives at the bottom of the sea
It has six more arms than me
A giant squid is slimy and wet
Do you think they're good at a poker bet?
The giant squid is rarely seen
It's much, much larger than a lima bean
This is the end of my squid poem
Now it's time for me to go home

Time
by Conor Nehl

Days whiz by, people are born and others die
Time is fast, we were just in the past
The air used to be fresh and clean, now it's full of gasoline
We used to be riding horses, now we're riding in our sleek black Porsches
We try to pursue the time we have been through
All the time we have went, has been spent
Look there are our footsteps to see where we have gone
Traveled and traveled but what went wrong?
The world changes in time, even right now as I say this rhyme
Time is everything; time is money but it's not always funny
Time can be sad and also bad but time can be fun; too bad we're all done
Chasing our dreams with our gigantic schemes
All around the world but time twirled and twirled
All my time is done but you're still there, so just keep playing in the sun

Sea Lion
by Megan Rulli

Down in the murky caves
Where there are soft, swaying waves
There is a squid sleeping peacefully there
He should ever beware
For there is a sea lion that's tan and light
He leans over and takes a bite
Right behind, he sees a gray shark
He darts and misses with a colorful spark
He goes right back
And proceeds on his track
He flutters off to the little light
And softly says, good night

The Hunt
by Stephanie Wagner

Deep into the pine forest where the river lays
Bluefish swim with brilliant scales, the moonlight on the waves
The elk and deer come down to drink the water crystal clear
Gracefully leaping over logs they take a quick sip, finding a predator near
The wolf comes out of his stone lair
The smell of his prey reaching his nose, gently trotting to the river
Of his presence no one knows, now the hunters being hunted from up in the sky
The wolf saw the dragon's talons stretch and knew that he would die
So the dragon hunts the wolves and the wolves hunt the elk
No one can stop the food-chain, hunting's what it's all about

Love
by Taylor McFarlane

Love is like the sky above
It goes on and on; it's never gone
For when hatred is near, we still have our dear
And when they pass on, they still won't be gone
For their love lives on in our hearts and souls
So when you think you're lonely, think of this
Love lives on forever ...

Friends
by Brandon Henner

Friends are nice; friends are cool
I like friends; they make me laugh
My best friend is Rory
I make two cookies; my friend gets half!

Wild Horses
by Amy Desjardins

Wild horses running free
Going where they want to be
Running under waterfalls
Going where the gold leaves fall
Rolling in the summer grass
Fillies playing as a task
Through the mountains high above
Leaving what they used to love
To prairie fields they go
They'll fill their stomach as they mow

Fishing
by Adam Trammell

Fishing
Fun, family time
Cast, reeling, hook out
Helpful, relaxed, happy, excited
Hobby

Beauty
by Shannon Peters

Crisp air
Trees glare
Yellow flowers
Everywhere
Purple one
Bright, yellow sun
Beauty will stare

Dream of Imagination
by Cecelia Young

Wind whispers in certain moments; what does it say?
Who is saying it? It's a big mystery to you
Is it a fairy, a unicorn, a half human, half chimpanzee with its first newborn?
Or is it just your imagination? That thing you use in your mind and in your dreams
You can imagine something peaceful, adventurous or dangerous
Plus many more ... you can create a whole world once you free your mind!

My Cat Lucky
by Ilana Hagaman

Crazy cat, insane animal
Cute, fuzzy, nice, loving
Mean, hatred, bites, scratches
Licks, purrs, orange, white
Smells bad, broken tail, runs away
Short haired, makes me laugh
Cute nose, pink ears
Meat eating on road, likes tuna

Coco
by Grant Mulzer

Coco
Dumb, stinky
Biting, licking, scratching
Mean, weird, cute, nice
Running, caring, sleeping
Sweet, loveable
Disney

Confused
by Katelyn Baird

Twist, turn, thinking hard
Annoyed, screaming inside
Ears ringing, people gone wild
Quiet, peace, calm, humming birds
Singing, silent

Super Stunt Boys
by Chris Callejo

Me and my friend Aldo are always doing silly-willy things
But my teacher Mrs. Manno, who likes the Sopranos
Dislikes the plan with the bike
We were planning to jump over the school
And land in a big, fat pool
We wouldn't get hurt, there's just some eels
Who know how to play "Deal or No Deal"
Let's ditch the witch!
We're already rich
Now let's go home to our flaming dome
And play with some Floam
I hope we don't burn
Or we'll have to squirm
To the Floam
That's the end of this poem

Waves Rolling
by Sam Perkins

Waves rolling up the sand, my feet getting soaked
The water freezing my toes off, tide pools by our cabin
Have anemones and tiny shrimp
I walk there with my family, but only with one or two people
At the rec center I swam the night away; I went water teeter-tottering
High diving, low diving, and rope swinging
The lifeguard giving out rules, the water shimmering like a sparkling ocean
Water exploding into the air, then I go back down into the sand of the city beach
The ocean like a huge bowl filled with water and life

Yawns
by Austin Thomas

There are yawns in blossom; they're blooming like big red roses
There are biffer-boumbirds making their nest
But how do they do this big job without making a blunder
They're making them up on the drawbridge at the castle of Krupp
If they don't fall asleep, there will be a big slumber party in the castle of Krupp

I Feel Sick
by Corissa Ambrose

My head hurts; Mrs. Manno is funny
She's making me feel sick, but she's as cute as a bunny
My stomach is queasy
I feel kind of needy
Mom got me a banana
So I could feel better and play with my friend Savanna
I went sledding yesterday and jumped over a ramp
That's what made my stomach hurt, now I can't go to camp
I feel kind of bored
I tripped on a cord
I fell on my knee
And man, I couldn't see
I told Mrs. Manno my stomach hurt
But she still told me, "You have to work"
She said, "Wait a while"
And a couple of hours later, I had a big smile
At Art, my head hurt
It could have been the smell of the marker or the smell of my shirt
Today it was just my stomach and my head
When I get home, I'm going straight to bed
I have a long way to go before I get home
But I feel sick and want to be alone
At the end of the day, I felt good again
But on the car ride home, I got annoyed
Because my sister wouldn't stop counting to ten
When I got home, I remembered I had homework and had to study
But my mom was being kind of nutty
An hour later, I was watching TV
And then I remembered Mrs. Manno didn't give my pocket dogs back to me
But I didn't worry
I knew I would get them back tomorrow; I'm not in any hurry

Friends
by Chloe Ibanez

Always there for you
Bring joy everyday
Cheer you up when you're down
Do crazy things sometimes
Every day is a special day
Friends are forever
Get along
Having fun everyday
I love my BFF
Jealousy never happens
Keeps your friendship going
Leave a smile on your face
Make you laugh at their jokes
Never bails on you
Once a week a play date
Perky princesses
Quirky queens
Racing you at recess
Saving you from trouble
Tell you secrets
Using special languages
Verses each other at games
Wish we will always be friends
Xplaining to each other our homework
Yelling just to be loud
Zoned out at sleep overs (Not)

Spring Is Near
by Kallie Rae Jones

Sprinkling water on the pretty white, purple, blue, and yellow flowers
Plants sprouting in the cool, light breeze with the hot, hot sun shining
Rainbows coming out of the sky after the long rainy days
Incoming birds flying as fast as the winds below will take them
Now that spring is here, I am getting excited
Grabbing all different kinds of flowers for the nice colorful vase

Dogs
by Brittney Bendik

A great playmate
Being a good licker
Chasing you
Digging in your garden
Eating all your veggies
Feeding young
Getting in the way
Hiding from thunder
In their cage waiting
Joining you in walks
Kind to each other
Licking your face
Man's best friend
Not listening
Outside playing
Playing fetch
Quitting for water
Resting and sleeping
Sniffing each other
Teasing you
Under the deck we go
Venturing around a valley
Water waters
X-tremely fun
Yielding when you say so
Zoning

Summer Fun
by Jesse Russell

Sailing lessons down at the beach
Under the pier catching crabs
My birthday
Making sand castles at the beach
Eating hotdogs from the grill
Riding my boat in the great South Bay

April
by Kristin Schmidt

A wonderful month
Presents for May
Rainy days
I love April
Lovely, lovely flowers grow

Halloween
by Mickayla Cleek

Hallows' eve is so naive
A good Halloween to you
Love is needed for a horseshoe
Love is needed for you
Oh, that scared me
When you look like Cindy Lou Who
Eh, I'm here with you
Eh, I'm scared with you, too
Now it's turkey giving

Teachers
by Trinity DeWitt

Teaching children every day
Education is their hobby
At home, they teach their kids
Checking worksheets night after night
Helping kids fill their brains
Every year pushing kids harder and harder
Researching at night to learn more about geometry
Smiling the whole day through, smiling at you!

The Wonder Boat
by Alisa Bedrov

Far away in the great big sea
Somebody's sailing without me
But do I care if I'm on it or not?
On that lovely big boat
Then it comes closer to the land
And the people can hear its lovely band
And now I wish they would sail with me
Farther and farther into the sea

Since Sally Moved Away
by Sarah Parker

Since Sally moved away
Roller coasters aren't fun, ice cream tastes horrible and people are mean
Since Sally moved away
Sunny days are rainy, thunderstorms are sunny and summer days are like winter
Since Sally moved away
Going to the beach is boring and going to school is exciting
Those are my days since Sally moved away

Starlight, Winter Night
by Reiley Porter

I lie down, staring up; winter wishes on a star
Starlight, winter night, on the wishes that I wish
Please let the stars shine beautifully
Please let me have the time to watch the winter stars above me shine

3rd Place

Gabriella Elfezouaty

For Gabriella, family comes first. She may often be found spending
time with her brother and sister, swimming, ice skating,
horseback riding, or enjoying another of her favorite sports
like volleyball or gymnastics. An accomplished pianist,
this talented poet is also an aspiring actress who loves the theater.

Peace
by Gabriella Elfezouaty

While I walk on
The shore of the beach ...
I wonder
What life could be
Out there in the sea
While the soles of my feet
Are tickled
By the tides
Each footstep wakes me up
To the beautiful ocean song
That calls me to it
With the perfect sunset
I am filled with joy
I find myself sitting on the sand
Watching the sun's last rays
Sink below the horizon

Emily Sickles

*An active fifth grader, some of Emily's hobbies include
playing softball and soccer.
In addition to her fondness for books and poetry,
she also loves music and is committed to developing her talents
as a drummer and as a pianist.*

*I Am Free
by Emily Sickles*

*The presence of dew
On the daffodil
The sky and I
Lay silent and still
The sunlight weaved
Between the trees
Tiptoed outside
The gentle breeze
The petals shed
And blanket the ground
An eagle soars
At the speed of sound
The robin on
The apple tree
And me
I am free*

Samantha Baloga

Samantha is a fourth grade student
who does well in school
and enjoys reading a good book.
Creative writing is one of her favorite pastimes
and she is particularly fond of poetry
as she feels it allows her a great deal of freedom.
It also seems to come quite naturally to her.

The Park
by Samantha Baloga

The sun is setting
Colors of magenta
Periwinkle
Violet
And bright yellow
Like an artist's painting
I stare for hours
Three little girls play tag
A puppy alongside of them
I hear laughter
As they call, "Molly!"
The pond is as clear
As the day's light sky
An elderly couple walk by
Hand-in-hand
Laughing at memories
They once shared

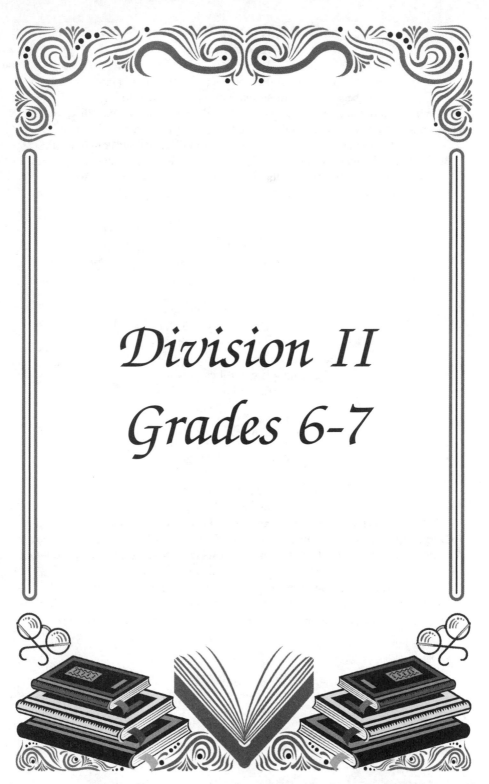

Division II
Grades 6-7

We Try Not To ...
by Breanne Martin

What would you do if somewhere in life's bitterness
You became something that you never aspired to be?
What would you do if you found out that all along you had been lied to?
What would you do if you began to realize that all of your fantasies were just a joke
That you could never handle? We try not to fall out of our day-dreams
Because it is the hardest thing to face, the reality are feelings that break us up
So we look around and see that we all get a chance to hold the world
But when it is our turn, the world changes into something that we do not want

Schools
by Mica Hollingsworth

The schools so rule
Friends are there but no one would care
They hate school; I say let's duel
I love thinking, my grades aren't stinking
Education is for me, can't you see?
Learning is great, I can't wait
For school

If I Could See
by Morgan Galang

My life is hectic; it is a burden
By the way, everything goes
When my mom makes orders and my dad makes shouts
Everything goes wrong, 'cause my brother fights back and my sister complains
All I do is sit and watch, when my ears are blowing, with tears going down my face
When everyone is still arguing and shouting
So all I do is run upstairs and cry out everything in my mind
But by the next morning with bags under my eyes, I find everyone hugging
All smiling and laughing, knowing that everything will be okay now

Life
by Tori Winebrenner

The only thing short about life is life
So just have fun
Because you never know when you'll be stabbed with a knife
Or shot by a gun
Ran over by a train
Or hit by a car
Get a tumor on your brain
Or in a fight at a bar
So overcome all of your fears
Do the impossible just for fun
Wipe away all of your tears
No matter how bad it hurts, you're never done
Just remember when it comes to life, you can never have enough time
So just have fun, even if it doesn't rhyme

Untitled
by Talia Berday Sacks

Spring's eternal hope
A bit of a rainbow's rays
Windblown and filigreed

Halloween
by Amber Mccalment

I love Halloween
We make slimy, spaghetti strings
I love Halloween
We love the things we bring
I love Halloween
I love to scream on Halloween

Life's Path
by Gus Sargentini

Sometimes people waste their lives with the violence of guns and knives
If only they knew the result, maybe then would they revolt
It seems they find out too late, after they've entered the prison gate
What this life can do to you is very cruel but true
If you get locked up, your life will be done
Thinking of your memories will not be fun
You may wind up sad and depressed
Prisoner clothes in which you are dressed
If life's test you fail, you may end up dead or in jail
Living on the streets is not cool; it's better to stay smart and go to school
Follow life's path on the one that is right, not the one that's nearly in sight
So let this be a warning to all that are walking life's path but ready to fall

Stallion
by Kyle Elliott

I am a black stallion racing through fields of green
I run down a hill with my mane fluttering in the breeze
I soon hit the sandy floor with the waves lapping at my hooves
As I leap over sandcastles built by a child, soon my journey ends at a stop
But now my spirit will guide my courage and strength for the long journey back

Looking At the Stars
by Lauren Stavroff

Looking at the stars, it's not hard to see the tremendous beauty of the world
But sometimes when it's dark at night
And the rain drips down from the angry sky like a star's tears, I wonder why?
Why must we hurt the world with our so-called ingenious ideas?
We kill so much for so little; what's the point?
Can't they see the wonders of the world are fleeting?
Why can't they see Mother Nature isn't to be bargained with?
Learn from the trees that bend in the wind; learn from the animals, how they blend
Learn from nature's children and find peace
See the way they interact? Can't you see?
They listen to the call of the wild
Do we have the authority to crush them with a single blow? No
Looking at the stars, it's not hard to see

Me, Myself, and a Stranger
by Kennedy Tunstall

Why do I always see myself living in
Other people's
Shadows?
Changing what I say and do
Afraid of what they might have to say
Them rejecting me when I am myself
The person they like is a stranger
Living life through my eyes
I am still in there
I can feel it sometimes
My heart is still pumping
Beating
And thumping to me
My heart is mine and only I can control it
Maybe the stranger and me
Are more
Alike
Than
We know
It

Life
by Lindsay Brett

As I wonder the question in my head, thinking in school or as I lay in my bed
What will happen tomorrow? Or the next day? Or the next day? Or the next?
But ... When you think about it, why care?
Just live life to the fullest and make everything fair
Don't cheat your way through life, it's not right
And you will regret it one lonely night
So, as I lay in my bed or think in my seat
I wonder how to live tomorrow nice and neat

The Dying Rose
by Molly Ayres

If you ever leave this earth, on your deathbed be you
If you ever lose strength, and faith is far down the road
If you hold on to me then I may be able to comfort you
If you had not brought me here, then I would not want to be born
If the wind had color and the mountains were agile
If water had texture and time had sound
If peace ruled the land like a shining king
If fate was as it seems then that is when I will stop loving you
If you were not in my life and I had never known you
If you knew what I would be like, you will never leave me
I need you more than anything, to be loved when comfort is needed
To have someone to celebrate all the riches of this world
If to think I will never see you after this very special moment
If I was to know that you will be gone forever
I would weep for the world, knowing that I would lose
Someone so special to me, my dear mother
Your hand slowly slips away and I think to myself, "If I let go, I am giving up on you"
I rest my hand in yours and wait
A single tear drops from my eyes onto your lifeless hand

Flying
by Rebecca Falleur

So you're soaring through the sky feeling beautiful and free
Taking time to notice the little things of life
Flowers blossom, seasons change, but you still feel free
Alone in the sky, being anything you want to be with the world at your feet
You reign over all for just one moment
You smell the wind as it brushes through your hair and there isn't a cloud in the sky
You see all of the happiness, love and joy in life, and forget the rest
Nothing could make this moment, this one moment in time, any better

Dream Land
by Megan Dean

Has there ever been a time in your life
When troubles and heartache cause you strife?
When all you wish is to find a place
Where all your cares can be erased?
I know of times such as these
And a place I can go when e'er I please
This place I know of is quite in reach
That's special to all, every, and each
A land where all my desires are there
I go there often, after my prayer
I can see high mountains, a comet, oh my!
But these I can see only when nigh
Now you may be asking, "How can this be?
Tell me this place I can be so free"
I tell you no lie! There is no twist
I'll tell you about it if you insist
This magical place where all can dwell
Every woman and man, boy and belle
A place that's nothing short of grand
This is the place, the place of Dream Land

Will You Always Be There?
by Brandy Brown

Will you always be there when I go to sleep at night?
Will you always be there when I sit and watch TV?
Will you always be there when I go to school each day?
Will you always be there when I lie in bed at night?
Will you always be there even when I forget that you're not?
Will you always be there even when you're gone to a better place?

What If
by Bryce Wanbaugh

What if the sky was green and the grass was blue?
What if cows said quack and ducks said moo?
What if cars could fly?
What if the president was the cable guy?
What if dogs could fly?
What if there was no sun in the sky?
What if dead people were sill alive?
What if two plus two would equal five?
What if TV was never made?
What if our memories were to fade?
What if this was all true?
What if it was? What would you do?

The Fellow
by Ian Smith

There once was a fellow, his name is Yellow
He liked yellow Jell-O; then we went to his house
Then met his mom, she liked yellow Jell-O, too
She made a lot of yellow Jell-O
Then I met his dad, he looked like Jell-O
That's when I met the fellow who liked yellow Jell-O

Bouncy Balls
by Raymond Jensen

The door opens to my shadowy closet
Everything is clearly seen because of the glow from the sun
The first thing I see are bouncy balls, surrounded by clothes
Small, multi-colored and round, some are dazzling, the rest are pretty
Their colors pop out, showing the joy that can be felt on this day
They are special to me and they fill me with happiness
They are fun and cheerful, remembering is just as joyous
But the one thing that has changed because of these balls
Is the happiness in me, in my friends, in my life

Smiles
by Kelsey Stickler

People always say, it takes more muscles to smile than to frown
But by giving people smiles, you can make their day when they are down
Smiles are contagious in never-ending supply
So flash a smile at someone as you walk by
If you give a smile away you'll get one right back
Smiling keeps you happy so there's no need to slack
So keep on smiling, then you'll see all that they can bring
They bring love, they bring joy, they bring many other happy things

Baby's Breath
by Miranda Fay

Baby's breath, sweet like the flower
In the great wind's power
The fragrance flows through the woods near a stream
As smooth and silky, like coffee cream
The sleeping baby is in her dreams
Who knows what she sees
Maybe bunny rabbits hopping around
The baby hears no outside sound
Her breath is steady and moves with the beat
Of that little drum inside her keeps
Her heart beats a tune, in the cradle she rocks
To a timer that goes tick-tock
Maybe one day the golden treasure she keeps
Hidden inside, still asleep
And will bring joy and laughter to everyone
Now unknown what her future will hold
The baby with her heart of gold

A Day In Nature
by John Hochgesang

Look outside at the trees
Waving in the breeze
See the golden leaves on the ground
Waiting to be found
Hear the chirp, chirp, chirping of the crickets
Rustling in the thickets
Look out at the owls
And hear the coyote howls
Hear the monkeys screech
And see the lion reach
For his next victim
And watch the fish swim
Watch the fox creep
Then suddenly leap
Watch the rabbit bound
Trying not to be found
Try to count the insects one by one
Until the day is done

The Children Who Suffer
by Luis Hernandez

People in Africa but nobody cares
People die every day and no one cares
A lot of children don't have parents
And a lot of parents lost their children
Everyday, more children are abducted
Some are even killed, some are forced to kill
If they try to escape, they will be killed
Some of the children starve to death because there is no food
Some children only eat one meal a day and that is all they do
Some people cry and some people pray
But never give up because all this will change one day

Alone
by Christopher Maldarella

As I walk home, reviewing the day
I walk all alone, no one with me, no way
Not many friends at school, not many laughs to be shared
But the plain truth is, no one really cared
No friends to call, just homework to be done
I just continue this routine and it's not too fun
I dread going back; I don't want to go
No one would truly miss me, it's the truth, I know
An outcast, a loser, a freak so I have heard
Or even more simply, just a nerd

Ode To Lobster
by Jordan Ponzetti

Oh, lobster caught in a cage, cooked and served on a plate
You're the best meal for me, you fill me up quickly
When I crack you the sound brings music to my ears
As I take my first bite, after I dip you in butter
I want so much more; without you there is no other kind of seafood

Ode To Sushi
by Werner Naegeli

Mmm ... sushi
Chopsticks are positioned, ready to dig in
Oversized sushi rolls to big to fit in my mouth
Wasabi tingling my nose
And the salty soy sauce gliding down my throat
Lemony, refreshing sushi, like Heaven on my tongue
Dozens of pieces of sushi, like a rainbow on my plate

Alicia Keys
by Kristen Thomas

There once was a girl named Alicia Keys
She's known as the queen of R&B
She grew up very poor
But that didn't stop her from wanting more
In New York, she went to the School of the Performing Arts
There her teacher, Miss Azia, saw she was smart
She learned to play the piano and sing
She worked on her sound and everything
She inspired me to play
So I practice night and day
On my birthday in Chicago I saw her perform
I loved all her songs, and she played all night long
I got a feather from her costume
And it will be me on stage one day soon

A Friend
by Ariel Weiss

A friend is someone who is caring
She would stand by your side making sure you are not hurt
While the others might laugh
A friend is someone who protects you
She will stand up for you in any situation
While others would just pretend nothing was wrong
A friend is someone who is trustworthy
She will listen and keep your deepest secret
While the others would spread it around the world
A friend is someone who you have memories and laughter with
You'll laugh your hearts out over funny situations that have happened
While the others would question and wander off
A friend is someone who understands
She will help you get through any crisis, no matter how big or small
While the others won't care about your problems
A friend is someone who is special and you should not take her for granted
You should give that friend everything that they have done for you in return
I don't know what I would do without friends

How's Life?
by Carrie A. Byrd

Having nightmares all about the bush
Getting brainwashed, something the parents didn't wish
Killing moms, dads, sisters, and friends
It's just like this war will never end
Let's think about it, children outside and they might die
They try to hold it in, but they have to cry
But did you know that they keep their spirits up
Praising God even though their life is rough
Everybody wants to live in the U.S.A.
They try so hard but the pain won't go away
A little girl having to be a grown man's second wife
This just isn't the right way for her to live her life
The rebels like to take kids 5 to 12
They all act like they don't, well
So for now on think about the kids that eat once a day
And those of them starving who pray and pray

Alex
by James Briley

I have a boxer dog
She's a big couch hog
Because she sleeps the day away
Alex likes to run and play
When she goes in her kennel, she gets a treat
At dinner, she gets to eat leftover meat
She sleeps on the couch and she sleeps on the bed
She sleeps anywhere she lays down her head
She sits, she lays, and even shakes
Alex and I, best friends we make

Religion
by Max Van Diest

Throughout my life I have discovered a very confusing thing
This term that used to have some meaning is used without consequence
A term that has been taken over, a term more like tradition by those who act
"Religious" or otherwise say they're "Christians"
If the term "Christian" means Christ-like and so many people use it
How do you know the difference of those who are only "religious?"
Because it's so very simple, you must understand, for Heaven's sake
"Religion" is what man made and what God made is called "faith"

What Happened To All the Superheroes?
by Dakin Macgowan

What if I were to tell you I saw Superman ... ?
Or Spiderman ... ? Yeah right!
Since when have we had some 'web-crawler'
Or a man 'faster than a speeding bullet'
Flying around the city, saving the bank from bank robbers?
What happened to Spiderman; did he run out of web?
Do we have so much kryptonite that Superman's afraid?
Or do they not care?
Maybe our town needs a superhero; who knows?

D
by Erica Cipollina

Somewhere in Heaven he sleeps on the clouds and dances on rainbows
Somewhere up high he thinks about me and watches over me
Like my protector, my guardian angel, my amazing ringmaster
And my mighty pirate mate, my crazy dancer and my grandpa
Somewhere he smiles and looks upon me
Somewhere he sings and dances and I'll always remember
Those singing words I heard the day of his death
"D" is now sleeping with God in Heaven

Ocean of Time
by Alexandra McHale

Ocean of yesterday, I loved you as a child
I longed to be your mermaid and travel through the wild
My buckets stole your shell-littered sand, and piled it on the shore
Your mighty waves pulled it back, but I came back for more
I wondered what creatures dwelled inside you, deeper and deeper within
Strong breezes blew my sun-bleached hair; your salt burned my skin
Ocean of today, I'm the teenager waiting at your door
School is closed, books are returned; I need to be with you once more
Ready with a friend, towel, flip flops, and song
You make me feel loved, with a place to belong
Thank you for a million shades of blue; for colliding with the sky
I promise to return and grow with you; share time as it gently slips by
Ocean of tomorrow, why do I worry so? Why is there regret?
You are as beautiful and mysterious as the day we first met
Yet, I know too much, read too much, you are in danger - don't you see?
You have given unselfishly, but man has taken too much, including me
Your life and our future are at risk; global warming threatens the Earth
I vow to protect and help you, friend; you have taught me what nature is worth

The Frowning Man
by Brandon Hough

There once was a man named Joe; everywhere he went, he frowned
No matter what or whether something was funny, he still had a frown on his face
Anyone he went to face, any place, in a frowning contest he beat them
But finally somebody beat him; the next day Joe smiled and he made friends
After that day Joe was happy for the rest of his life

Before They Were Married
by Brenden Owens

He wrote her love letters
With every note, his love swelters
He never could get her off his mind
Until the night he would find
That she would never
See him as anything better
So he vowed to get her off his mind
After that, he was doing fine
But that was before they were married
She accused other people of loving
Her and her love to him was fading
She found that every note had clues
One of them said he liked the blues
Her boyfriend knew who it was
The only reason he told him to stay away was because
Then she gave up before the night
He stood up for her in a fight
So she kissed him good-night
But that was before they were married

Halloween
by Gina Renga

It's coming, the wind growing heavier, changing, darker
Light disappears, ghosts return to Earth
Jack-o-lanterns give them a scare; graveyards hold the flesh of the souls
The night's grim falls into the hands of ghosts and goblins
Oh yes, have fear because on this night they're very near
Don't stay up too late; why, you ask?
If you see the Reaper it will be your fate
The barrens of the underworld gates are open wide
Would you like to take a peek of what's inside?
The vortex of ghosts and goblins fade into the night
Don't worry, you will be one when you see the light!

Rebels
by Halie Davis

The sun goes down
Hospital floors fill
Screams of pain are heard
As brainwashed children kill
Hospital basements and bus parks overflow with helpless children
Awaiting for another long night to end
Schools are entered
And more young ones are abducted
Packed together like goods
They all wish for the sun to rise
When the light shines above the horizon
The small fighters go back to the bush
Hospitals empty
Children fill with relief
But when night comes again
The rebels return

Hardship Lives
by Alfonso Mack, Jr.

Africa
A sad place in the world
Where children get shot
Their parents die of AIDS
Children have no homes
They don't have any phones
Rebels kill
Rebels steal
Rebels have AK47's
Children die like it's 9/11
I wouldn't want to live in this place
Children get shot in the face
They starve to death
They live underground
Why do they live so bad?
Do they need love?
Let's help

The Clueless Girl
by Cami Hall

There was a clueless girl; she was the dumbest girl in the world
She had the greatest mother, too; she finally knew
What was going on; her mother was the saddest one
Her father didn't have a clue
He didn't know what he was missing; he was missing all the kissing
But the most important thing that he was missing; the one thing
He threw away his life, but most importantly his wife

My Life In the Bush
by Stephanie Sumption

In three months I saw six hundred and forty people killed
And two thousand children that were abducted
So far there are fifty thousand children that are living where I live now
Where I used to live, children would sleep in hospitals
Because they feared that they would be abducted by the rebels
Just like I was at least five years ago
Sometimes we would only get to eat once or twice a day at the most
And sometimes I get bad headaches if I don't see blood
I've been learning how to shoot for at least five years now
I don't even remember my family
Some children ask me, "Don't you fear the rebels?"
I just reply to them, "Yes, most of the time I do
But if you do as they say, then you have nothing to fear"

Penguin
by Norberto Maldonado

Carnivores
Mostly eat krill
Thick layers of blubber
Black back, white front
Penguin

Celebrating Fathers
by Vera Spencer

A little child is like a limber leaf, singing and dancing in the wind
Makes such a vision to sight, as flies a father's love
With the light pointing straight to you
All we have of freedom, all we use or know, this could be a journey for us
You never know, someone might care to wander from his own friends
You're as happy as can be because there's no where else to be

Life
by Neeli Rhodes

Life is a story of choices and trial
It may have some downs but is fun all the while
We all make mistakes and from them do we learn
We do what it takes and rewards we must earn
A person decides what he feels is right
Some do not speak up, while the others must fight
We all have our good times, our worries, our strife
And all of these aspects together make life

All In This Special Room of Mine
by Sabree Chandonnet

I wish I had a room but not an ordinary room
It would have horses and sheep
With a clear, glass ceiling in which to look at the heavens
And it would have a big, green rug with a massive, king size bed
And a huge television with a PS3 videogame set
A gigantic stereo system and a Sony laptop computer
With an ice snow cone machine and a big fireplace in the corner
With a little, puggle puppy named Josephine and a mini refrigerator
All in this special room of mine

Ode To Chocolate
by Kyle Nelson

Chunky chocolate so, so sweet
Melts in my mouth when I want to eat
I am so happy with its silky taste
When I am around it doesn't go to waste
Once I see the color brown
I start to laugh like a clown
Once you're gone I want some more
If I don't the rain will pour
When I chew for all to hear
The scrumptious sound goes in their ear
They're jealous they can't have a bite
Even if they try to get some with all their might
My nose can smell you miles around
You are the sweet smell of success that can be found
Your rich cocoa goodness I hope is nearby
If there wasn't chocolate, I would die

Spring
by Lawson Gutzwiller

Blooming flowers pop up in the ground, not a single sight of snow is around
The sun is shining so bright, this is a good day to fly my kite
It is good weather to play outside or maybe even go on a bike ride
Everyone is out and ready to go; in the garden sits my dad's hoe
Children playing at the park; the sunshine brings out a monarch
The little butterfly flies in the sky, up, up, so very high
I could stay outside all day, run, swing and just play
Spring is my favorite season; do I have to give another reason?

The Bull Fight
by Dylan Karr

The door opened wide as the bull ran out
Full of pride, they teased him and made him bleed as he hurt in every limb
Then out came the matador, shining in the sun so bright
Running out from behind the door, he took his cape from his shoulder
Waving at the bull like bait, he stabbed him with his sword
And he fell down dead, then he was tied up with cord
They ran him around the ring so big as the dead bull was bound

Ally
by Jamie Flock

Other kids wonder, why is Ally so sad looking? The teacher says she will be alright
Ally starts to weep at school everyday, then she starts to pale and cough
One day she coughed up blood, the next day, Ally's weak
Monday morning, she does not show; the kids ask where Ally is
The teacher replies, she is alright now

Odd Pets
by Andrew Biller

My elephant has no trunk
My giraffe is three feet tall, there's no spray inside my skunk
And my poodle has no jaw, my squirrel's tail isn't bushy
My mouse has a tail of thirty feet
My cat's ribcage is all mushy and my goldfish, you won't want to meet
My porcupine isn't spiked, my parrot has one wing
My zebra isn't striped, and my beautiful lark just won't sing
You might say I have some weird pets
But amazingly the vet
Says confidently in one line
"They are odd but they are fine"

Ode To Kiwi
by Amanda Cytowicz

Oh, kiwi, you seem like a mini coconut to me
But when I cut you open, you are very green
You smell like a tropical punch
When I eat you at lunch
You are fuzzy, soft to the touch
I enjoy you oh, so much
You taste sweet, sour and fruity
Also very juicy
And as I slice you open, I hear the loud chops
Then all of a sudden, everyone stops
Then I ate you; a burst of sweet
And I jumped up on my feet
Without you I might go crazy
I'll eat you often; I won't be lazy

The Five Nights
by Shanna Preston

On the first night, rain drops fell on the little girl's head, "More rain today," she said
On the second night, the stars twinkled in the sky
The little girl went to play out in the moonlight
On the third night, the clouds covered the sky; "Two more days," the little girl cried
On the fourth night, the moon shone in the sky, "One more day," the little girl sighed
On the last night, the little girl woke up in a white room in a golden city
"I'm finally here," the little girl said

Ode To Gum
by Tom Demling

Gooey, gooey, oh so chewy, even though you're a little screwy
I hear you pop when you get too big
You taste so good, you smell the best; I love you when I'm taking a test
You're better than an apple pie; I hate to have you when you're dry
You're like a roller coaster in my mouth; I love you more than life itself
You feel so good on my face; I can see you a mile away

Friends Are Important
by Kathleen Friedrich

Friends are important in life
Life is like a little kid touching water for the first time
Time is a river flowing
Flowing of canoes down a twisting river
Music is my rhythm in the morning
Morning when I awake
Awake on a beautiful day
Day so bright, it puts a smile on my face

Dog In the Fog
by Jason Hawes

When some people see a dog come out of the fog
They hope it won't fight them or even just bite them
They hope it will just leave them alone
When I see a dog come out of the fog
I pet it, and if it's nice and I didn't get bit
I'll give it a bone

Roller Coaster
by John Trainor

A roller coaster ride, waiting in line
You get in, the bars slowly slide down
And you slowly go up the steep drop, and the suspense as the front leans over
And the waves of hands shoot up like rockets
And then we all go over blazing fast down the drop
And the girls shrieking, and the loopy loop
And the flips, and the click, clicks of the cameras
And the dark tunnel, and the slow stop
And the buzzing sound to get out and the bars slide up
And the ride is over

The Sky
by Christi Wolgemuth

The sky so high
It's as blue as can be
As the clouds go by
I slowly sip my tea

Memories
by Amanda Levy

She looks out her rainy window
Window of viewing the past
Past of forgotten memories
Memories never returning to what used to be
To be replaced in her future
Future to have an excuse for hope
Hope is like a bird in the sky, it's free
Free to go back in time to change
To change fate
Fate figures its curious destinations
Destinations determines destiny
Destiny is her future

Guitars
by Conrae Johannes

Guitars come in many shapes and many forms, some bass, some acoustic
Many with tone whirling whammy bars; some so old they even have battle scars
Just like snow flakes, no two are the same; a few of these axes even shoot flames
Amps blast, speakers sound; guitars rule the world

Summer
by Colleen McWilliams

When the summer comes, it brings a lot of flowery mums
Kids are off from school and they love to jump in the pool
The day is a peach when you get to go to the warm, sunny beach
Parents soak in the sun while kids are having fun
Kids are selling lemonade; when they're done, they see how much they made
Dogs are running around and digging in the ground
Summer is so much fun; the kids are sad when it is done!

The Butterflies
by Natasha Redlin

I turn around and see your eyes
All I feel are the butterflies
Floating in my stomach about to come out
But the words spoken are merely my doubts
I know I'll regret this falling in love
Because living this lie is just proof
Of that the truth is the truth and lies are lies
These are the feelings of the butterflies

Springtime
by Emilea Hill

It's warm outside but it's cold in here
I can't help but love this time of year
Leaves on the ground, buds on the trees
I'm starting to see more butterflies and bees
School's almost out, no more time to study
No more hair that is wet or shoes that are muddy
Since there's no school, we can play all day
How about hopscotch? We can have a relay
The sun always shines; there's no cloud cover
Only white, puffy clouds; over my head they hover
For me, springtime makes everything more beautiful
It makes everything prettier and more colorful
When it's sunny out, the grass seems greener, the sky more blue
Everything seems to be pure, everything so true
Now you can see why I like the weather
But between you and me ... I like summer much better!

Stare and Wait
by Timothy Foley

I stare and wait, I was many thing
Scared, confused, curious, worried
I see my mother there
Then giving me a hug and a photo of us together
I noticed she was leaving fast, she hurried
She left me with my aunt who I really appreciate
The my mother left, giving me her love and faith
I do not know what to do
So I stare and wait, stare and wait

Invisible
by Jena Chapman

These invisible children, these invisible tears
Lead children to face terrible fears
Of losing each other and families, too
That they use hospitals as a tight fit drawer
With no mother beside them, no teacher to school them
That the fear of abduction leads them to sleep on the floor
And if they stay home, what a terrible price to be in a war as children
And when they are rescued, they can't think twice without seeing blood
They go mad, all the war and the killing
Think of the invisible children and the fear they go through
But there, where war is fought by kidnapped souls
Like a night without stars and brainwashed fouls
Others hope, others dream, that war will cease and peace shall rise

Out of All My Moms
by Joanna Davis

Out of all the moms I've ever met, you're the one I won't forget
And if I die before you do, I'll go to Heaven and wait for you
I'll give the angels back their wings and risk the thought of everything
Just to prove our friendship is true

Deceived
by Gauri Shastri

They told me they're cool and the ones all see
And if I were like them, the star would be me
To a foreign country, I went that day
My true self going farther, farther away
Life used to be so sunny and bright
Now I've lost my sense of wrong and right
Suddenly, it snapped right into my brain
That I acted wrong; that filled me with shame
That I should feel proud of what makes me, me
For there will never be another person like me

What Is Peace?
by Emily Sherman

What is peace when there is war
And death comes knocking on your door?
What is peace when twin towers fall
When terrorists have come to call?
What is peace as the soul reaper nears
Gnawing, clawing, out your fears?
What is peace? Global warming is close
Because of pollution some fear the most
Peace is a world without crime
When darkness and evil are frozen in time
Peace is a baby's silent slumber
As crickets play their chirped-out number
Peace is happiness, and you may find
That you'll receive it by being kind

Ode To the Road
by Corey Ertman

Road, oh road, this is your ode
You get me here to there; you show your rough side with your concrete coat
You look so elegant with your little strips
Along with the people, bikes, and cars floating over you
With no idea what's in store
Road, oh road, you're the best
Some forget your wonders, some wish to discover your infinite secrets
But no one can truly figure you out
Road, oh road, you strut next to the sidewalk forever
You will always lead somewhere, but where you lead is the true wonder!

Knitting
by Jesse Horney

Yarn, yarn, everywhere I see
As I sit in my wooden rocking chair I try to decide what colors to choose
I chose red and blue because they are cool and I like them a lot
As I start I hear footsteps coming my way, but it's only my cat coming to play
He rolls around here and there playing with the yarn
Now he's tangled so I have to stop for the day
And help my cat escape from the bundle of yarn
Must also untangle my yarn, which isn't really fun
But on the bright side, I had a good day
And, if I can get the yarn untangled, I hope to knit again someday

Beau's Pain Inside Me
by Makenna Childers

Beau hurt me deep inside; the pain gets stronger all the time
The hurts gets deeper and I don't know why
What can I do to make it leave? If you know, tell me, please!
I need an answer, but where can I go?
I've asked a lot of people and they don't know
I have a lot of questions just for you
There are a lot of people I could ask, but no one like you
What should I do? Where should I go?
Beau, I need you; my heart is broken without you
I feel a hole inside me; a pain within me
Help me, I need you

Risen
by Shannon Lowery

All the stars in the sky He made for me; all the sand on the beach, how can this be
That my Lord would die for me? They nailed Him to a cross on Calvary
Satan laughs and cries with glee while soldiers mock and cast their lots
On the third day He's been dead His disciples cry with dread
But when they see He is risen they leap and sing, "Hallelujah" to their Lord
One will not believe unless he sees; Jesus appears and all is well
Jesus ascends and all will tell; Jesus has risen from the dead!

A Killing Memory
by Gurnaina Chawla

Tell me ... where is the peace we all yearn for?
The lives of the innocent and the success of hardship, all lost
What did it show? What did it prove?
The feelings they never got to share
The ideas they never showed let out
The abilities they never recognized
Enormous daggers of pain
Slowly and torturously sliding itself through people's hearts
Can't we all love? Can't we all hold hands like brother and sister? Can't we share?
The lies that turned to tears, the pain that turned to depression
The small objects obliterating mankind
When peace is achievable, why must we kill? Why must we hurt? Why must we lie?
The lives of others lost, nothing but a memory
A memory itself ... that kills
- Dedicated to the honorable people who lost their lives on April 16, 2007 in the
Virginia Tech. Tragedy

Ramesh Ramsaroop
by Andre Ramsaroop

Ramesh
Funny and wise
Relative of Andre, Dad
Who likes to work in New York City, watch western shows and movies
Who feels happy and strong
Who would like to see Toronto, Canada and the Caribbean
Resident of New York
Ramsaroop

The Casket of Death
by Matthew Stone

One, two ... it was in the afternoon ... I got confirmation
That my grandmother was dying
Three, four ... got home ... my mom told me that Grandmother had a bad sickness
My brother knew that she would last only for a few more days
The next day she passed away
The wake was that day – it started in the morning
Five, six ... that day ... my twin brother and I went to the wake
The first thing that I saw was the casket
Because it seemed so different to see one of your loved ones in a box
It was almost like seeing yourself in there
I wanted to cry, but I couldn't
I wish this could all go away ... but it can't
Seven, eight ... everybody is feeling emotional ... some people were crying
Hard as water falling
It was very sad for three people ... my dad and his two sisters
Nine, ten ... the final word was being said ... and everybody said their last prayer
After that people left the room –
They, too, began to cry
At the burial ground we all threw a rose onto Grandmother's casket
And said our good-byes

Winter Wonderland
by Victoria DeRosa

The swirling vortex of white snow curling around my toes
It's all flat and white until tonight
Then I go outside, I see not a piece of green in sight
It's like heaven on land; it's a winter wonderland

The Sun
by Danielle Schmal

The sun
Its clouds are twirling and swirling
The sun is very bright
Can't see it at night
Gives us a lot of light
27 million F - very, very hot
Cold it is not
Medium sized star
Very, very, very far, far, far!
The sun is hotter than 1 million cheetahs
Blazing, twinkling
The sun

Tears of Joy
by Peter Marino

Winter is a happy time, a cold time, a time of joy
Snow falls from the sky like magic; little white sprinkles fall to the ground
On the ground is a blanket of snow
White snow and on the snow footprints lead to the heart of a blanket
And there lays a small child waving her arms rapidly in the snow
The child is laughing with joy
The child's laughter brings tears to an old man
Sitting on a bench in the yonder, crying tears of joy

A Painted Picture
by Victoria Landin

A sunset is a painted picture
Smeared with vibrant colors
Vivid ruby, crimson and maroon
Radiant gold, saffron and canary
Brilliant peach, tangerine and pumpkin
And dazzling plum, violet and magenta
A sunset is a painted picture
Smeared with vibrant colors

There's the Bus
by Jake Arthurs

Honk! Honk! There's the bus
I got to go, I love Mom
I love you too, when you get home come help us
Ok, I yell, after I play with Tom
I hop on the bus and take my seat
I get out my Game Boy to play
I think of our lunch today, pizza with breadsticks of wheat
I look outside, it's a beautiful day today
We stop at the high school and kids get off
As I watch them leave, I start to cough
When we get to school I take in a breath and ...
Heave! (Very heavy backpack)
Fin

Summer Is Coming
by Wesley Whitman

Summer is coming at last
It feels that the sixth grade has gone so fast
We already have passed the first day of spring
Soon we'll be having the school bell ring
I can't wait till we get to go to the city pool
Man, will that water feel so cool
I hope the summer days will be fun
With you, your friend and the sun
But if you sometimes want to be alone with just you
There are many summer activities you can do
Don't worry, the wait isn't too long
Just don't try to do anything wrong

A Poem For Her
by Chelsea Beard

I sit in my bed and I wonder what went through her head
She came and went just as fast as Lent
I miss her so; why did she have to go?
It was like a murder or a killing; it sure wasn't thrilling
I held back my tear; I couldn't hear
That she was now in a better place, although I couldn't face
I couldn't stand that no once could lend a hand
To help me through my pain; it was such a shame
All my dreams would not come true and I couldn't get through
The wall that was holding me back, I could not lack
Now she is gone
It's almost as bad as it is sad
She practically committed suicide
But I know she is in a better place, so I will just have to face
- Dedicated to my late Grandma Clark

Procrastination
by Zane Rathgeber

Off in the future, I will complete it
Until that day, I won't do it
Without a second thought, I won't do it
In a drawer, I will stuff it
Under the bed, I will throw it
Throughout the day, I pray for it to stay
For tomorrow I will have to complete it
Against my will, I am forced to do it
Before I know it, it's done

Autumn
by Ellie Thompson

Autumn is a beautiful season
A season when the glorious colors
Of red, orange, and yellow drift from the treetops
Crunch, crunch, crunch! The sound of the leaves being raked up
Jumping, leaping, soaring into piles of leaves
Crackle, crackle, crackle, the leaves under you
Rake them up all over again
Summer is long gone, autumn passes quickly, winter is ahead

Billy Reid
by Anthony Marchetti

Billy
Good cook and funny
Relative of Anthony, cousin
Who likes cooking, games, and homework
Who feels happy and loves his family
Who would like to see Green Day in concert
Resident of New York
Reid

Heaven's Gift
by Nicole Mojica

Love is pink
It sounds like wedding bells ringing
It smells like a rose
It tastes like strawberry ice cream
It looks like fluffy cotton candy
Love feels like a kiss on the cheek
Peace is white
It sounds like doves chirping
It smells like a vanilla flower
It tastes like white chocolate
It looks like puffy clouds
Peace feels like a warm blanket

Ode To Root Beer
by Joseph Meyer

Oh, Root Beer, your bubbly taste
Let other sodas go to waste!
Yet if I drink you too fast
You'll sting my nose with a sugary blast
If you were to leave the planet
I would just take Coke for granted!
Please never leave
Because of you Root Beer, I can believe!
Mug and A& W are the best kinds
And the good thing is, that you can pay in dimes!
Your sheer goodness and creamy delight
I can drink you day and night!
With ice cream, you make a float
When I drink you, other's gloat
Your smell, as good as bacon
I will get you before you're taken!
Root Beer, you are my god
I worship you day and night

What is Green?
by Kathleen Moloney

Green is the color of a stem on a rose
And green can be painted on a lady's toes
Green is the color of a pea in a pod
And green can be the favorite color of God
Green is a part of a rainbow so high
And when a tornado comes, green will be in the sky
Green is the color of leaves on a tree
And green is the color of the wide open sea

Dependant On Plants
by Rachel Halversen

What would life be like without plants?
No more leaves, not one swaying tree
The view is as plain as can be
No more bushes, no home for the birds
No longer can the sound of chirping be heard
No more flowers that bloom in the spring
No more sweet smell that all flowers bring
No more fruit that grows out of trees
No more pollen to be collected by a bee
Without carbon dioxide that comes from plants, too
How would we survive, what would we do?
We need plants and I now understand why
They make our world beautiful and without them we'd die

Nature
by Asia Smith

Oh, we see all of the green trees
And the beautiful colors of the rolling seas
The colorful leaves of nature's ways
Is the beginning and ending of nature's days
Orange, yellow, and also red
Are the right colors that God said
All the rustling of the colorful leaves
Will make you want to say, "Be quiet please!"
But that's okay, 'cause it's still a pretty sight
For most of you, the rustling's alright
The colorful seas of nature's ways
Is the beginning and ending of nature's days
Different greens and different blues
Are the right colors God said to use
All the swishing of the calming seas
Might make you fall down to your knees
But soon you'll get right back up
'Cause, some creature or human will interrupt
The colors remind you of the space above
And the sounds remind you of all the love

Can You See It?
by Brianna Johnson

Can you see it?
Can you see the loneliness, hurt, pain?
Can you see the heartache and the tragedies?
Do you see all of the lives that those people drain?
Can you see it?
Can you see the tears that don't fall?
Can you see the fear that is inside?
Do you see the strength put into it all?
Can you see it?
Can you see the hunger they have?
Can you see the help they crave?
Do you see their souls enslaved?
Can you see it?
Can you see how they're brainwashed?
Can you see how their dreams are tossed?
Do you see their self-esteem lost?
Can you see it?
You may see it but they feel it; help out

Not Me
by Corlee Osborn

When I look in the mirror, what do I see?
I see a person who is not me
I do not know who this person is
But she is definitely, definitely not me
Because when I look in the mirror
What I see just isn't me

Heather
by Carli McCormick

Heather, as you sway alone in the dark
Making sure it's all right for you to go in the Lord's arms
Your beautiful, golden hair swaying, longing for the wind
Your gown flowing like a misty breeze
Don't go away; stay, stay and play
I know I said goodbye and said I would be alright
But I'm not, so please stay as I watch you go in the light
The person who was there is gone but the memories still cling

When My Mother Died
by Margaret Tully

The darkness faded in
My whole world just caved in
I sleep and sleep all night long
My mother I dream of as I sing a song
She is pretty and wonderful in every way
I just can't believe she died today
Her eyes shine in the sunny light
As we buried her body at the grave site
She lies there still all alone
Until an angel carries her home
Away she goes up in the sky
I still can't believe she died last night

The Lost Ones
by Emily DuBois

Inspired by the Wal-Mart missing child posters
We are the lost ones; we can't speak for ourselves
You need to quit pushing us back on your mind's shelves
We are the lost ones crying out from this wall
And we wonder, "Do you care at all?"
We are the lost ones, posters ask, "Have you seen me?"
But you walk on, "Have you no feelings?"
We are the lost ones, but we can be found
If everyone a little more effort will expound

The New Hitler
by Derek McDowell

What spawns evil?
Is it lust? Is it revenge?
No, it's not ...
It's hatred
Joseph Koney ... the man of evil
Evil is rarely seen in our world
But when it comes ...
Is it not our duty to fight it?
Are we not "the protectors of peace"?
Joseph Koney has committed atrocities against humankind
Hatred has pushed Joseph Koney so far
That he hurts others that have nothing
To do with his cause
Everyday, he forces children
To kill and to torture
We only joined WWII because we were affected by it
Isn't America supposed to help everyone?
I give a call ... to humankind ...
To fight the new Hitler

Children
by Jessica Kolecki

Boom, boom! Gun shots go off
Parents and kids lay dead, while other children are hiding in a basement
Children crying at the thought of death; children get abducted everyday!
Children getting killed by rebels at the sight of crying
Little kids sleeping four to a bed, eating one meal a day, if that
One hundred and three degrees outside with no air conditioning
Ladies prayed and did chants for the lives and children
Kids drawing pictures of wars and fighting
Brainwashed ... children woke up early on a daily routine, not that they had to
Neglected ... all children and adults want is peace
Death ... two million people died! Bring peace!

Wish
by Jordan Allen

A wish is a dream you want to come true
You can wish when you're happy, you can wish when you're blue
Wishing is hoping and believing in fate
Don't worry about the time, it'll never be too late
Wish to reach your dreams because they're never too far
Look up into the dark sky and wish upon every star
Wish when you're young, wish when you're old
A wish is in your heart, it's not an object you can hold
Wish you were a super hero and had the power to fly
Wish for everyone to be happy, then no one would cry
Wish for world peace and sadness to be gone
Wish for winters to be short and summers to be long
You can wish for anything, anytime, anyplace
Wishes are dreams you must be willing to chase
Wishes are yours and only for you
No one can break them, and only you can make them come true

Can You Tell Spring Is Here?
by Michelle Rowland

Feel the air, no more cold or death
There is me at my window in a stare to see the birds frolic
Look for food, bathe and drink on my pool cover
See the statue of Saint Patrick shining its last in the sunset
Spring is full of life and resurrection, love and willingness
Cleansing and purifying, rebuilding and reconstruction, can you feel it?
No one pays attention to it, our home is slowing
The squirrels funning and digging for their nuts
To be disappointed in not finding them because we dug them up in the fall
Fall is fun, but it's a sign of tiredness and dying
We use violence to solve everything; even a fly by swatting it or a bird with a gun
The birds may be loud and interrupting but it's music to my ears, can you hear it?

Last Day of School
by Mary Shaffer

The bell rang at 4:05
The kids yelled and laughed with pride and joy
We got on the bus, and the teacher had a fuss
And nobody knew why
She said, "Ok, at least it's the end of the day"
And we all went on our way
Whoo hoo!

Pointe
by Sarah Taylor

Toes bleeding, pads sliding in your shoes
Blisters for beauty, pain for elegance
Sore legs forever and ever
It's wonderful to the eye, brutal for the legs and toes
Toes bleeding, pads sliding in your shoes
Blisters for beauty, pain for elegance
Delicate toes hitting the floor
Legs stretching hard, toes going numb
All of the pain that beauty becomes

The Spirit
by Michael Reed

Watching Heaven's surface, bunch of clouds of white
Would I be the most beautiful spirit watching people down below?
How would it be? Close as I can be to her
Always touching her, I could watch Heaven's surface

I Hear America
by Allison Marotta

I hear America crying for the fighting on our land
I hear America crying for taxes no one can understand
I hear America crying for the men that we have lost
I hear America crying for the shortage of food and cloth
I hear America crying for the representation that isn't here
I hear America crying for the lies that are still unclear
I hear America singing for the truth that has been received
I hear America singing for the faith in which we believed
I hear America singing for our homes being restored
I hear America singing for the victory we have scored
Singing with open mouths, their melodious songs

You
by Emily Fields

No one knows who I am
Everyone hates the one called, "It"
Everyone laughs, then everyone screams
Everyone but you
You never laughed, you never screamed
You always stood there
Holding me so no fears would come
You always said that everything will be alright
You never hated, you always cared
You ... Thank you for everything you've done

Winter
by Ashley Bernstein

Zippers zipped, buttons closed
Snaps snapped, lips blue with cold
But open wide at the beautiful sight
Of winter wonderland frozen in the moon's silvery light

Spring Is the Time
by Noah Hill

Spring is the time when life reawakens
Spring is the time when flowers burst forth from a long winter's nap
Spring is the time when the sun appears once more
Spring is the time when all life is reborn

A Moment
by Melonie Christopher

A moment may be walking past someone you like who doesn't know you exist
A moment may be slightly sweeping against the arm of a crush
But it means nothing to them
A moment may be when he catches you watching him
But it won't even change anything about what you two have
But the true moment is when your eyes connect
With the one you think you love, then know you love them
Your eyes will connect, you both will smile and think the same, "I love you"
And the true moment is when you feel like your world is perfect
And you never want perfect to end!

Poetry In Me
by Meghan Gamble

Poetry dwells in me
It's around me like a bird waiting to be heard
In between my toes, it squishes as I walk
Creeping up under my skin till I burst out with song
It cries for me and cares for me; it calms me on a weary day
Becoming my storm on paper as I bleed and bleed with agony
To somehow, some way, put those careful words on my paper
Into place, without mistake, those precious, simple words of poetry

Skate the Day Away
by Sam Griepenstroh

Skating the day away, the day goes by fast
I kick and I flip like a jumping bass; I swish and I swash down the ramp
The wind in my face, I love to go up and down the ramp
When I wreck, I try again; when I make it, I let out a grin
I love to swish and sway like a bird in the sky
It's fun to skate with a friend; it is fun to skate by yourself
It is fun to practice new tricks; it is fun to play follow the leader
There are all kinds of fun things you can do when you are on a skateboard
I love to pop ollies, it's as fun as can be; I love skateboarding and that's just that

Fun
by Florence Adamis

Fun is singing with a bird
And playing with the herd
Fun is playing games
And praying to God
Fun is saying jokes
And never smoke
Fun is being silly
While playing with Willy

Dory's Truth
by Jaclyn Brennan

I really have no memory loss, I just like to swim
And when I verse Marlin, all I do is win
Nemo has no lucky fin, they just used computer animation
All toilets don't lead to the drain, they're just used for elimination
Marlin speaks one language, but for me I speak two
Maybe if Marlin spoke more than one, he could talk to you
You know I speak English, but I also speak whale
Now you know my story, so I guess I am finished with my tale

How Could You?
by Christal Schmucker

How could you let all this happen?
How could you allow sin and death to be part of us?
How could you leave your children to suffer?
How could you bear to see us shed a tear?
How could you let us live in pain and agony?
How could you bear to take all of that for us on the cross?
How could anyone blame the one who created them?
How could anyone live without praising you?

Favorite Book
by April Hampton

My favorite book, it's off the hook
It's also very funny; man, it is also hot and sunny
It is at a beach but with a bad leech
It talks about jokes, about some folks
This book can be gross if you hate toast
You've got to read this book because it's off the hook
You don't want to miss out or else you will start to pout
So read this book or else!

JoAnn Murray
by Kevin Murray

JoAnn
Beautiful and intelligent
Relative of Kevin, mother
Who likes to work at Shop Rite
Who feels a strong commitment to her family and everyone should be nice always
Who would like to see a better world, a better place
Resident of New York
Murray

Basketball
by Marty Weiss

Basketball
Bouncy, colorful
Jumping, shooting, flying
Reaching toward a goal
Rucker Park

Ode To Pearls
by Katie Cooke

You're as delicate as the slightest treasure
Starting as just a grain of sand
What a glossy pleasure
And you make a classy strand
You are a vast foam ocean
Racing through my veins
Escaping from my clutches
You're rolling down the lanes
Oh, dear pearls
One day I'll pass you to my daughter
And hopefully the string
She will not slaughter
Happy memories will bring
Of long ago beach trips
Where the sandy smell still lingers
And gulls still ringing in my ear
Such a special sense
Of luxury you cast into my heart
Oh, dear pearls
You are my beautiful, innocent art
My dear pearls
Please, stay together
As you're skipping from your hand
In thirty years the string will tether
And those pearls won't look as grand

Spelling
by Tyler Durfee

"My teacher is mean, " said a kindergartener one day
"She makes us spell hard words like hat and ball and hay
She keeps on adding terms, until I feel quite sick
Then she forces us to memorize them quick
I've spelled bat, cold and hot and day
I've spelled sat, old and pot and way
I've spelled can, ham and even spam (whatever that is)
All of the words are too hard for me!
Go easy", I plea!
A second grader said to her
"Your words are easy, I wish mine were
I have to spell words like take or care
Hope and that and even lair
King, wing, thing and sing
Rope, nope and char
My words are harder by far"
Then a fourth grader yelled at him
"When it comes to spelling, you'll never win
The words get harder the older you grow
I, of all people, should know
My teacher makes us memorize words
Which no one else has even heard
Things like theater and getting and lung
Knights and Saturn and even done
Planets, return, movable and more
The words cover the entire floor!"
A high school student walking home
Overheard them and said, "I've known
Many children being foolish, it's true
But this is the most I've seen in one school
You see, words like bat or king or even knight
Are far easier than what I have to write
I spell words like Gettysburg Address
Hydrogen, nuclear, and cardiac arrest
The words you have to rehearse
Will only get worse

Babe
by Morgan Johnston

A slow glance at me and I felt sad; I knew what was happening
My sweet Babe was leaving forever; her eyes messy and sorrowful
Her legs weak and tired and her heart failing
As the day coming home from camping is still clear in my head
It is the day I never want to forget
"Babe ran away, she might not be coming back"
My heart sank; tears fled from my eyes
Ring, ring, ring; my aunt answered the phone
As I hear crying from downstairs, I wondered about Babe; was she found?
She hung up the phone and called my mom at work
My mom was sobbing on the other line
"Babe died, Chris found her in the ivy in his backyard
She got in a fight and was too weak to fight back"
I hung up the phone; my eyes sorrowful
My legs weak and tired and my heart sinking

War
by John Gavin IV

War is a monster
Its roar is a gunshot or a clash of steel
A ceaseless moan and the ever mourning of a family's heart
Ever killing, ever crying
Ever lasting war

Clouds
by Shannon Letscher

As I lay in the grass, I look up to the sky
To see all the clouds go by, and it makes me so calm
I look up to the sky to see my emotions
And it makes me so calm; I'm relaxed inside
To see my emotions, one would never know
I'm relaxed inside, and everything is right
One would never know, to see all the clouds go by
And everything is right as I lay in the grass

Summary

Summer
by Shelby Deller

The sky is blue and light
The sun is hot and bright
Into my suit I go
Thank goodness there's no snow
Dive into the pool
Aaah! Now I'm cool
There's sun and suits
Parades and flutes
A nice browning tan
Vacation time! Hop in the van
Going to the pool or even to the beach
All the way to the rope I will reach
My Popsicle drips down my chin
I wipe it off and my mom hides her grin
Summer's almost over, back to school
New middle school will be so cool!

Untitled
by Rachel Fogel

Floating o'er the surface of a pond
The petal croons its lazy tune

Baseball
by Derek Mulzer

Baseball is one of the greatest sports; baseballs are soaring through the air
Balls hitting the wooden bats; the bats crack and fly through the air
They run to the dugout to get a new bat; they try to hit again without a crack
Bam! The ball flies through the air; he runs around the bases like lightning
They throw it from the outfield to home; the runner dives at home
The ball is coming into home; dust is in the air from the base runner
Everyone is waiting for the ump to make his call
Here it comes! Safe! Everyone yells in excitement
The team jumps up and down from the victory
Everybody goes home and talks about the game
The next day is normal and the day goes on
The team has another game and the fame goes on

My Past
by Luke Jackson

Standing firmly on the ground, but I'm falling, falling into darkness
Memories gush back like a raging river, tears shoot down my face like bullets
Bruises re-appear upon my body; the pain you brought me
Every mistake I made, your fists clenched
You made me think cruel, cruel thoughts
Thoughts that told me death was the only answer
But friends got help, they told me things would be okay
The next day I watched as the policemen took you away
You might have been gone, but the pain will always be there
Then I saw your eyes, the eyes that will burn in my soul forever
The eyes that told me you'd be back, waking up in a cold sweat
The nightmare is over until tonight, where I relive my past once again

The Chase
by Lainnie Alexander

Sometimes I wonder if it's all worth it, if going after you isn't gong to be wasted
I realize you don't know that I chase you, how hard I try to keep away from you
I wish you could love me, but nothing can do
What I want you to see, what I want from you; my heart beats fast, I wonder why
You cannot hear it sitting next to me; besides, I must give you up, how I don't know
For now I realize that I love you so; you know I exist but just barely in this game
But you don't even know my first name

Friendship
by Breeanne Babe

Friendship is hard, but also loving
There are people that share and friends that care
People who are ungrateful and some who are faithful
They can be loyal; they can be cruel
Sometimes friendship is a battle; it is fought with fists and guns
More often, the most effective weapon is a simple act of love and courage
Be a good friend in everyday life
Do all that you can to defend in the fight

Untitled
by Christopher Nordhoff

Warm winds kick up winds
Blossoms flower on huge trees
Grass grows tall daily
Rivers flow through woods
Leaves fall into the river
Snakes slither up trees
Many birds soar high
Big clouds grow darker very fast
Insects duck from rain

Fresh Spring Air
by Connor Shields

Evening's darkening sky made up of the varying ginger and golden sky
My nose caught the scent of the freshly thriving flowers
My eyes saw the scene of stunning mountain top trees
My feet loved the feeling of walking on fresh sod-like grass
I loved the sensation of the fresh, spring air
I loved how it feels to just run outside into spring
After a ruthless and malicious winter
The feeling, the unbelievable feeling of being able to jump outside
Run around and melt away in a fresh pool
It is so astonishing to see the flowers and scent the air
After such an incredibly long winter all cooped up inside

That Stupid Emotion
by Krystal Clingler

The heart breaking, hand sweating, tormenting
I want to be with you forever
Never say never emotion
Shared between two people is the unbelievable
"What is he or she doing" emotion
That hard to get rid of emotion
That annoying, that irritating emotion
That wonderful emotion
That, that, that incredible emotion of all things
Is love

Springtime
by Andrea VanPelt

It's springtime and the flowers are blooming
New growth everywhere
And there's so much to be doing
Colors as bright as a butterfly wing
Swaying teacup shaped flowers
Give us a reason to stop and sing

If I Were a Can of Pepsi
by Jessica Cimino

I would clang down the road as I roll from the wind
I would smash into people's heads
I would get thrown into the sewer
I would drip down the can
I would be shaken all up as a prank
I would sweeten the mouths of children
I would swallow all the water for the puddles
I would be chilled on hot summer days
I would dehydrate you on hot summer days

Seasons
by Martin Craig

The sun is bright, right?
It is very hot indeed
Can't you tell it is?
I like bananas
They are very good today
I am a monkey
The leaves are falling
They fall in many colors
They fall in the fall
It is very cold
Is that snow I see, Koco?
Yes, it is indeed

I Really Do Love You
by Janett Trujillo

I want to hear your laugh, see your smile
For you to say "I like you," well, it might take you awhile
I will admit it that I really like you
I've even told my friends, I'm sure you don't feel the way I do
You've caught me at my weirdest, both me and my best friend
I'm glad I met you and I'm glad that I'm not dead
There are some things you don't know, if we get anywhere I'll confess
But for now it's better not to tell, you might think of me even less
I know I might as well be chasing a dream, one that probably won't come true
It might be too soon to say but I really do love you

The Magic Hat
by David Allen

The magic hat put the cat
In a hat with a dog named Elliot
With a belliot, with a friend
The bear named Bogar
With a sogar

Harmonies of Life
by Katherine Sexton

The harmonies of life
Good times and strife
Sickness and health
Poverty and wealth
Fears and delights
Early Monday mornings and late Friday nights
Frowns and smiles
Times when you're joyous or when grief's heaped in piles
Good hair days and bad
Happy times and others where you're sad
Energy bursts and lazy spells
Moments everyone laughs, some when they all seem to yell
Days when you feel carefree, others when your heart seems stabbed by a knife
These are the ever-needed harmonies of life

Jessica Young
by Justine Staggs

Jessica
Enjoyable
Super nice
Super duper
Invincible
Cat-like reflexes
Awesome

Young
Outrages
Understanding
Never-ending bundle of fun
Giant feet

Was
Active
Smiley

Here
Entertaining
Relaxed
Ending madness

Spring
by Nicholete Randall

Someone and I
Prancing over fields
Running and laughing while eating
Ice cream when we sit
No one else on that
Green hill but me and that someone

Jessica Lee Young
by Hayleigh Southwood

Jessica
Exciting
Super cool
Surprising
Incredible
Caring
All girl

Lee
Enjoying
Entertaining

Young
Outstanding
Understandable
Nice
Great
- Jessica Lee Young, my friend

My Teacher, Mrs. Scott
by Traci Longanecker

She teaches reading and spelling, too
Only late assignments can make her blue
She's never cruel and always cool
That's my teacher, the best she can be
She would read, run and rush us through
That's my teacher, the best she can do
Then one day, I came up with this

Mannerly
Respectful
Soaring into the future

Sending us on
Cool with Riverside
Out of this world
To make us learn
The joyous ways of reading and spelling

3rd
Place

Kaela Helmbold

Despite her poetic prowess, this varsity cheerleader
cites History as her favorite subject in school.
When she's not cheering her team to victory,
you may find Kaela keeping the beat
as her school band's drummer.
An active member of her scholastic leadership class,
reading, music, and dance round out this young lady's busy life.

Cherry Blossoms
by Kaela Helmbold

Cherry blossoms fade
Pink tears falling off gently
Splashing on the grass

Elizabeth Gaa

Elizabeth has devoted herself to academic pursuits
and should be very proud of her "A" student status.
Not surprisingly, this award winning poet is passionate about reading
and writing, with adventure/fantasy being her most beloved genre.
A clarinetist in her school band,
she has now taken on the piano as a second instrument.

Into the Rain
by Elizabeth Gaa

I am the child of the broken, the forgotten, forsaken
I live in the rut of desperation, alone in this wide, wide, world
With no one to love, no one to hold
And the rain comes down like the tears of all who have ever lived
Who have ever loved
The rain comes down in buckets, but it wasn't always rain
The sun once shone over me, a small child of the Ukraine
I had a family, a place to shelter me from the pouring rain; a home
All hope veiled by the rain; now I sit, sorrowful, alone
And the rain comes down like the tears of all who have ever lived
Who have ever loved
The rain comes down in buckets

1st
Place

Kendall Gedeon

While playing tennis and soccer
are among her favorite pastimes,
writing is at the top of Kendall's list
when it comes to special interests.
She does make time, however,
to practice playing the piano on a regular basis.
Her poem "Dreamer" is one of our top selections
and we found it to be very inspiring.

Dreamer
by Kendall Gedeon

The crippled boy who's rejected by all
He wants to become the next star of baseball
He knows that he can't, because he will fall
He's a dreamer
The little girl who will soon say goodbye
Knows she has cancer, and tries not to cry
But still she wishes on stars passing by
She's a dreamer
The mother who can't support her child
Has four jobs, but the pay is mild
Still each day she laughed and smiled
She's a dreamer
The father of two, whose wife has just died
Cannot bear the death of his bride
Still he lives on with hope and pride
He's a dreamer
The person who willed their ambitions to come true
Who fantasizes, prays, and wishes too
The person who has a different worldview
We're all dreamers

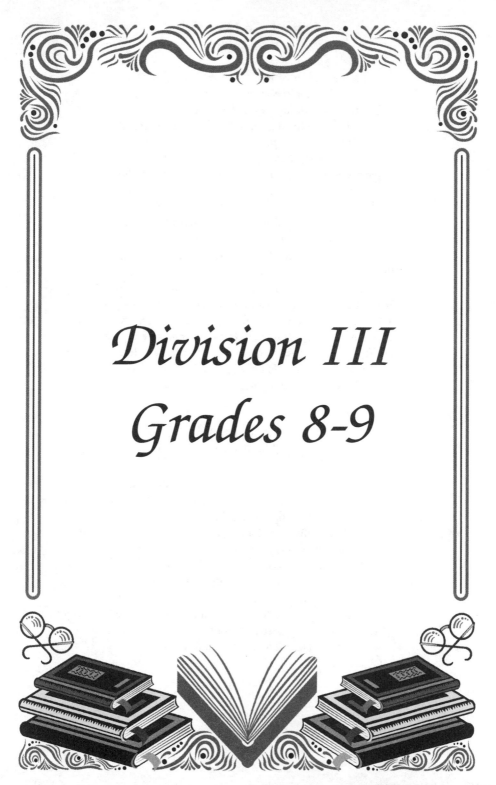

Division III
Grades 8-9

I Thank God For You
by Hillary Baize

It's the season of love (like we could forget)
Romance is in the air and it's making us sick
Couples are holding hands and all through the day
We walk down the halls and have to witness P.D.A.
Then all those girls will go home tonight
And thank God above for the man in their life
But when it comes down to it, we've got something they don't
Friends who'll be there when a boyfriend won't
Friends who'll be with you, there through it all
When you're feeling little, they make you feel tall
Friends understand when you want to stay home
No, you are not mad ... you just need time alone
When you're eating with friends, you can just dig right in
There are no guys around ... so who's trying to stay thin?
Now and then there's that urge to someday meet a guy
Who'll put a smile on your face and a spark in your eye
And someday it will happen but until that time comes
Take advantage of now and just simply have fun
So when other girls pray for a love that is true
When I pray at night, I thank God for you

Never Shed a Tear
by Morgan Phillippo

She knows not to cry, sometimes she needs to scream
Never knowing what she can say, she keeps it inside
She's the girl making you smile on your lowest day
She has all of her pain locked away, away in her heart and soul
No one will ever know how she feels today
Maybe tomorrow they will know
But again today, it will stay a mystery unknown
Unknown and all alone, no one will know today
She knows not to cry, sometimes she needs to scream
Never knowing what she can say, she keeps it inside
No one will know today

Together
by Stephanie Wood

Standing alone on a cold night, heart aflutter, filled with fright
Memories tell her she'll be alright; she hits the door with all her might
Upon his horses, alone they trot, followed by his absent thoughts
As she thinks of the love he brought, upon the night mushrooms rot
She sits down on her cold, damp bed, trying to think of what she's read
Wishing a veil upon her head, waiting for a man to wed
I followed the map of which I had, along the path I know is bad
Who sent me to find her is her dad, for she is the one I wish to have
I find her on the fourth floor; I knock on her wooden door
I say, "Here you are trapped no more"; together we will take flight and soar

Figuring It Out
by Lindsey Kohfield

How could something so right, end so soon?
How could something so beautiful, turn so ugly so fast?
How come our love didn't last many more moons?
How come our love didn't last ... ?
There are many reasons, but less than none
It must have been because I wasn't the one
It must have been her, excited and free
She must be the reason that you're not with me ...
How excited she must be; now you can both be excited
Happy and in love; how excited you must be now that you are free ...

The Out of This World Excuse
by Katherine Comer

Oh no! I don't have it! Is it due today?
I'm dreadfully sorry but I'm afraid it flew away
I was watching my grandpa whose fake eye fell out
Then I heard a buzzing and the room I looked about
My essay began to float away; aliens took my work, you see
As I watched with an expression far less than glee
So now I stand before you sounding like I lie
But just ask the aliens, they'll be my alibi

Who Decides?
by Casey Sulok

Cushioned and shining, Brazilian oak
With swirling patterns upon the arms, grooving deep then rising up
She sits upon this chair; she's the beautiful, young, polite woman
Rough and sandy, Douglas fir
Scratches and tatters on the arms and legs
Scars run deep but some only just surface
She's the typical, young, brash girl
It's in the eyes of the beholder
Which chair, which girl, which woman is which?

I Hear America
by Joseph Ferme

I hear America singing over its freedoms
The right to vote, to speak our minds, practice our religion
I hear America singing over opportunities
The jobs that are offered, good schools, good neighborhoods
I hear America singing over the technology and natural resources we have
But America's singing is being drowned out by its crying
I hear America crying over global warming
And the pains that come with it, such as skin cancer
I hear America crying over the cost and scarcity of fuel
That puts people out in the cold
I hear America crying over the war on terror
That ruins and devastates lives every day
I hear America crying for the homeless and the poor, and drug and alcohol abuse
And the attacks on 9/11 when so many lives were ruined
I hear America crying over abortion and gang wars
I hear America crying over murder and obesity
Immigration and pollution, AIDS and terrorism
I hear America crying and she's crying way too much

Shutting Me Out
by Amanda McTiernan

I'm at a loss, don't know where to go
Don't know what to do, what to say
I never thought, I always said
Never thought you'd end up dead
Inside you're crying, inside you're dying
Outside you're lying, not showing me all your pain
I tried not hurting you but you changed
I'm at a loss, crying inside and out
You changed so quickly, shutting me out

School-Yard Bully
by Justin McCormick

There once was a kid who thought he was cool
And he bullied everybody at school
But he got a surprise
When someone hit him in the eyes
And now he is not so cruel

For My Sister
by Emily James

For my sister
The one who makes a flute sound like a bird chirping
The one who has a strong, courageous voice
For my sister
Who wears clothes of how she feels that day
Whose posture is the best I know of
For my sister
The one who says, "Always follow your dreams!"
The one who tells me she loves me forever and always
For my sister
The one who always helps me through rough times
Who loves me for who I am, and not because I am her sister
For my sister
The one I love dearly!

What Does It Mean?
by Tara Mullin

Abduction, killing, what does it all mean?
It means the fear in one's eyes, the torture that goes on
Lives are getting ripped apart, families are torn apart
Fifty million abducted, twenty-year war
Two million dead of ruthless acts in the war
For a child, the rebels stand in their way
Chanting goes against abduction
After being abducted, there is no turning back
You will become a soldier
Joseph, spirit by day, abductor by night
To hide from him, you must sleep in a watery corridor
Is it really worth living for?

I Hear America
by Brian McCarthy

I hear America crying because of the unjust crimes that are being committed
Wars and the darkness of death has taken over humanity
I hear the cry so clearly as if she is standing at my side
And hatred lurks around and is growing at a constant rate
Tears hit the ground because of the provoked greediness of Americans
And how poverty would not be departing any time soon
I hear America singing because communities are coming together in peace and unity
I hear the beautiful voice of America because no child is left behind
We distinguish ourselves with the many opportunities that are granted to us
America is singing with great joy because we show patriotism to all we meet
We are fighting for our freedom, for ourselves, and countries in need
America sings for stars and stripes, through perilous fights
America will never stop singing because of the generous hearts we have

Slowly Drifting
by Sarah Shephard

Clouds; a delicate form
With great gracefulness
Are free to do what they please
They don't follow guidelines
Just the swift blow of the wind
Gently swaying away from Earth
Nightfall carefully creeps in
As the sky darkens
And the clouds disappear

Bad Relations
by Shannon Bales

Bad relations with him, with her; I don't know why, half of the time it's all a blur
Is it something I say? Something I do? Is it the way I look compared to you?
Bad relations, it's true; here and now you're not judged for the inside of you
It's brand names, it's your race, it's bad names, it's all over the place
It's social classes and pre-made thoughts because of a pair of glasses
Bad relations, it's because of you; so stop and think, I know you'll feel blue
Cliques and clans, you have no clue ... what you can do to others just like you

This Place Is Hell
by Kaylen Jaques

Stomach churning, eyes burning, I don't believe what I see
I feel so sick but it's not happening to me
People dying everywhere, sickness, sorrow and despair
Is the place you would call Hell; surely no one will be saved by the bell
Little babies being thrown into the air, mothers and fathers too sick to care
Here I am, hiding from everything and everyone, hoping, praying for just a little sun
If they don't find me, I might be saved
If they do find me, it will be the end of that day
If they find me, it will be the end of my life
I fear I am going to die; I ... I hear big, loud, monstrous footsteps
I am breaking out into a million cold sweats
Help! Help! They ... they're coming for me!
Stop! That's a wrap; we're done with that scene

Perpetually Lost
by Amy Tang

A little girl, all alone in the night
Flitting about, searching for some sort of light
And then from the darkness, a tune starts to play
And the little girl dances, dances the night away
Sometimes you just come across those days
When the music never stops, and the world fades gray ...
Dance away, dance away, away from life's commotion
Dance away, dance away, lost in perpetual motion
The sound carries on, carries her through the streets
Tap dancing, tangoing, ever so discrete
Gracefully bowing, and spinning away
Into the horizon as the sun starts a new day
Sometimes you just come across those days
When the music never stops, and the world fades gray ...
Dance away, dance away, away from life's commotion
Dance away, dance away, lost in perpetual motion

I Hear America
by Travis Simon

I hear America crying the overheated tears of sorrow and frustration
That come from disastrous global warming
Over the intensifying sun rays that are so damaging
Weeping about the thinning atmosphere used to store oxygen
And outraged citizens shouting out their severe untreatable diseases of distress
A war that seems to never come to peace
And people who break the laws and hurt others
With all the ones who have tried to succeed but never got the chance
But too, with all this crying, I also hear America singing
For happiness and joy, for their freedoms and independence
And the right to have a say in their country
And warm homes and food to eat during the gruesome winter
The happy children who can participate in school every day
For renewable resources that will help to eliminate pollution
And the great technologies being created every day
By people with awesome minds who want to make our lives easier and safer
Singing with an open mouth their melodious songs

Who I Am
by Jennifer Watson

I might not be perfect, but I'm worth listening to
I'm sorry that I wasn't ever good enough for you
I'm not trying to upset you or make you feel weird
But I'm trying to be myself and get to know you and me
I don't want to do this to you, but I'm gonna have to say
That you make me feel low and like I'm worthless all day, every day
You don't speak it all the time; your actions speak for you
Now I'm going away and never coming back
Away in a place where I'm good enough for everyone
Maybe one day I'll return and I'll be good enough, even for you

My Life Poem
by Nicole George

I am from a soft, cozy bed with butterfly pillows
From blue to purple walls
From a scent of cotton candy in the air
And a loud stereo playing Panic! At the Disco
I am from a loud, vibrant, joyful and fun place to chill
I am from the Big Apple to the Lady Liberty
From a huge park surrounded by tall buildings
From a very long island sticking from the east
And a place to see a great Broadway
I am from a state with many types of backgrounds
I am from a place where everyone unites and supports each other
From the Grand Canyon to Disney World
From hot dogs and hamburgers
And from different cultures and neighborhoods
I am from a country where everyone cares
I am from a free living country
From people helping one another
From doctors to nurses
And wonderful green land we can all share
I am from a future where everyone can get along

Homework
by Alex Miller

Homework, homework, it isn't fun; homework, homework, just get it done!
If you have something, something to say, say it right now; say it today!
Once you are finished, you can go play, but remember, tomorrow's another day!
Everyone hates it, nobody cares, and everyone thinks that it isn't fair ...
Get a good job, fix up your hair
But remember that homework, homework got you there!

I Still Love You
by Hannah Arnold

I want you to know that I still love you
Even though we are miles and miles apart
I still love you even though you had to leave me
And I understand that you had to depart
Even though I lay awake at night hoping you can see me
I need you to know that I still love you
I know you had no choice; it wasn't anybody's fault
I just wish right now I could see you one last time to let you know I still love you
All I can think about is the day when we can meet again
So I can tell you just how much I still dearly love you
- In memory of my mom, Valarie Lynn Arnold

Popularity
by Diana Pacinello

A girl sits and she cries, tears dropping down to her thighs
As she sits, she thinks how she went to the sink to do what she knew was wrong
For wherever she pleased, she goes and she heaves, just hoping to be 'fat' no more
After every meal, fat and ugly is what she feels, just because of what people say
She cries and she cries, pain stabbing like knives
For the way she gave into these people
A thought to be thin gave way to a sin and now she agrees that they're evil

I Hope We Meet Again
by Lindsay Hadley

When I first heard the news, I didn't understand
So you told me all about this cancer, while you softly held my hand
To see you so weak and helpless really did hurt me
You tried to stay strong though; you said you'd never desert me
The day that the chemo side effects set in, one of my fears came true
You had forgotten me; one thing you said you'd never do
When the horrible day of your funeral came, I couldn't make it a reality
But it's finally set in, you really have left me
I know you are in a better place, away from all of your pain now
And I hope we'll meet again, some way, some how

Take Me Back
by Mariah Hipskind

I miss you so much, it's only been a day
I cried and cried when I heard you say
"I love you, but I'm not in love with you"
I thought to myself, why, and how could you?
Things will never be the same, I keep hearing your name
Running through my head; my life is such a dread
I say to myself, everything's okay, "But it's not"
I need you here with me, I love you
You mean the world to me, I can't just be friends
I want more than that, what can I do to get you back?
I'll give, I'll take, I'll do, I'll be that one you always wanted me to be
Anything for you I'll give, please let me be the one you want to be with
I'm begging you, just let me try, to change what you saw/see in your eye

I Hear America
by Kristin Devine

I hear America crying and I do not like the sound
Though you may not see it, there are problems all around
The world is drenched in violence and treacherous animosity
And we are losing those we love from war and from disease
I feel America quivering in worry, though we're trying
To stop the world-wide problems, I still hear America crying
I hear America singing a song of happiness
And instead of showing hatred, we are spreading bliss
Diseases are being cured and poverty will end
When we put aside our differences, our problems begin to mend
I hear America singing in unity against the wrong
Singing with an open mouth, her melodious song

Remote Control
by Haley Beasley

If I had a remote control, I'd watch the sunset over and over with you
If I had a remote control, I'd replay the first time we ever kissed
If I had a remote control, I'd pause time when we look into each other's eyes
If I had a remote control, I'd fast-forward through every second I'm not with you
If I had a remote control, I'd go back in time and save you from pain and suffering
If I had a remote control, I'd stop you from doing drugs
If I had a remote control, I'd change only one thing; that we lasted forever
If I had one laugh to share and one breath left, I'd share it all with you

My Sweet July
by Megan Ryan

The fireworks, they boom and bang; the night is perfect; there is no rain
Don't you love it how the time flies by? Just breathe it in, my sweet July
It's August now and here comes school; we're draining out the swimming pool
I really feel that I might cry, my last breath of my sweet July
It's November now and it just snows; don't you hate how the cold wind blows?
I look outside; no more birds fly; I really miss my sweet July
It's April now, the first sign of spring; I go outside and hear birds sing
It's raining and no longer dry; soon I'll have my sweet July
It's warm outside at the end of June; my sweet July will be here soon
Don't you love it how the time flies by? Just breathe in my sweet July

Inside
by Angela Sharon

Inside lies a heart full of hurt and sadness
Inside lies a heart that has, for the second time, been engulfed in darkness
She lays crumpled on the floor crying
Screaming that she doesn't want to hurt anymore
Tears of pain and anger stream down her face, eyes that tell her forbidden fate
Outside she cries and screams, wanting somebody to come rescue her
She dreams of running away from all her pain and fears
She dreams that someday she won't lie crumpled on the floor
But she'll live forevermore without any tears
Tears of sorrow and hate roll down her face
Screams that tell the world to take her from this dreadful place
Inside lies a heart that's been torn since the day of that one horrible storm
Inside lies a heart engulfed in darkness with eyes that once had a sparkle
But now look dreary and solemn in her abusive life
Outside I lie on the floor wishing that someone will take me away from this war

Tremor
by Michelle Hy

Feet so tired, giving way; frigid moans pursuing ever so closely
Causing a tremor throughout my body; cold sweat runs down my cheek
Left, right, all a blur; I turn back, legs go numb
See nothing; a screech pierces the metallic cold
Ears bleeding, heart pounding, feet ... lungs failing
A gasp for air, can find none; slowly, surely, legs crumble
Woe's blade slits up my leg, a crimson scrape upon my skull
Turn around, last time, eyelids shut; one ... last ... breath
Holding sheets close in familiar warmth; a large, soft sigh

The Hunted
by Kyle Griswold

Heavy footfalls, the sound of my heart beating
I hear a dog barking, he's picked up my scent
I am running, running for my life
A shot is fired as loud as thunder, whizzing right by me and hitting a tree
I try to keep running but stumble on a log
I am running, running for my life
Then he's upon me, a knife to my throat
My heart is beating furiously as it begins to burst out of my stomach
I am done running, running for my life

I Hear America
by Kevin Gallo

I hear America crying
Pollution damaging our air
Contaminating our environment
Global warming, a concern for upcoming generations
I hear America crying
The cost of fuel is getting out of hand
Scarcity makes us anxious about the future
Terrorism has changed our lives
I hear America singing
Speaking their minds
Practicing their religion without persecution
Voting for their nation's leaders
I hear America singing
Our advanced technology aiding us to prosper
A higher standard of teaching
Educating the future of our first world country
I hear America singing
The efforts of our service men and women
Keeping us out of harm's way
Singing with an open mouth their melodious song

Friends For Life
by Elaina Black

Long summer days, messy ponytails, tank tops and shorts
Bike rides and tan lines, scraped knees, scarred elbows
And dirty hands with pink chipped nail polish
Bare feet racing across the ground, dirty toes, and the occasional splinter
Friends for life
Short summer nights, girl talk, prank calls, sneaking out but never getting caught
Chick flicks, ghost stories, camping out, all nighters, junk food
Sleeping bags, lightning bugs, gossip and shadow puppets, moon and stars
Friends for life
Through troubles and trials, you are my security
Secret keeper, corner stone, foundation, family
And friends for life; my sister

I Hear America
by Michael Hernon

I hear America crying
I cringe at the sound
It wails of people dying
Piled up mound by mound
I hear America crying
Of murder, bullying, and blinding
It wails of people vying
From promises that were binding
And yet in the midst of all this
Upon the corner of my ear
I hear things not so ludicrous
I hear, I hear, I hear
I hear America singing
Of prosperity, peace, and good cheer
If you listen, the sound really is ringing
With promise for a good year
It sings of justice and liberty
Of what it has become
All that extends to you and me
But most of all, America sings of freedom

What the World Owes Me
by Makenzie Lumsdon

When I lay on my bed, my eyes all dry
I feel a warm presence by my side
It feels so soft and comforting on my bed
Its whiskers twitched and its eyes were sad
The motor, it vibrates from its place
It's unique and different at every trace
And when I pet its warm, soft fur
The small animal didn't cease to purr
Her small meow echoes in my head
As I remember now ... that she is dead
My eyes welled up from the truth
For she was so young, only three
A small tear slithered down my cheek
As what the world owed me

She Is Amazing
by William Hix

Reaching eighty, old and gray; never thought I'd see the day
Mother lying in a bed, suffering a disease to death
Doctor said that she might die; this might be your mom's last night
I went to say goodbye to her, then she said her last words
"My sweet son, I love you so; one day later, I'll see you go
Son, don't cry for me today; I'll see you in Heaven with a smile on your face"

Let's Go
by Denita Scott

Your nerves are shocked, you don't know what to do
Step up to the line; get ready in your mind
Put your feet back, get ready; on your mark ... get set ... bang!
You fly, the wind picking up, feeling like you're in the sky
Wind hitting your thighs as you go, step by step, passing everyone
In your mind, you're saying, "Come on! Come on! Let's go!"
Hear the voices saying, "Come on! Let's go! Pump those arms!"
All the way to the finish, cross the line! Dang, I won!

While You're Gone
by Treva Bivens

I look up to the sky and often wonder why you can't be by my side
Why are you so far away and yet so close to me?
I talk to you everyday; we could be having so much fun
We would walk and talk and soak up the sun
But while you're gone, we can do none
One day we will be reunited again
But I will remember you always until then
So when that day comes, I will be ready to walk and talk and soak up the sun!

Remembering
by Chelsea Duehmig

Remembering the first time we touched
Is like saying goodbye and not knowing why
Remembering that first date
Is like seeing the sunrise on the beach's horizon that we walked so many times
Seeing you after our goodbyes
Is like seeing your best friend die right at your side and you are helpless
Remembering all the times we laughed
Is like realizing it will be our last
Remembering all the arguments we had
Is like watching World War II with your very own eyes
Seeing you in your deathbed
Is like experiencing death and then coming back to life
To realize your family hates you; realizing this will be our last everything
Our last kiss, our last hug, even our last laughs
Realizing that you and I are over is the worst thing I could do
So I am not going to think about it; nothing is wrong and I love you

The Tuxedo At Night
by Kara Barnett

Tux, the cat terrorizes the house; no one is safe when he is about
The living room is convicted, the kitchen is a mess; at night, he's quite a pest
He's dressed up every night, all in black and white

What the World Owes Me
by Jacob Greene

The world owes me someone to love
The world owes me someone to hug
The world owes me someone to miss
The world owes me someone to kiss
The world owes me someone that loves back
Someone who won't say, "Forget about that"
The world owes me an unbroken heart
One that is fixed with no edges that are sharp
The world owes me someone who cares
Someone to catch me if I fall down the stairs
The world owes me someone to love forever
Someone that won't leave me, ever

My Heart Is ...
by Sharrice Irving

My heart is being compressed by the spiteful men
That are captivating the world's juvenile lasses
My heart is being trampled by the vicious, erroneous endeavors
Toward the animals that are supposed to be loved and cared for
My heart is being compacted by the women
That are being convicted for the assassinations and abominations
My heart is being trodden by the egotistical administration
Towards the productively functioning Indianapolis Public School's students

Dying
by Emma Smith

Her eyes flicker; my view comes and goes
A tear rolls down my cheek; I see her start to cry
She reaches out a hand to me; her face feels soft and warm
I can't look away; our eyes connect
I let out a cry as her hand falls; no final words but the look on her face

Mom
by Cody Shannon

My mom is the bomb; she is loving and caring
She is helpful in all things; she helps me understand things
She is always there when I need her; there is nothing that she can't do
I believe in her every time she helps me; her confidence is overpowering
She is incredibly smart and talented; she is my mentor and confidant
She is my guardian angel and my best friend

The Moments of Lacrosse
by Danielle Peterson

On the field, all is forgotten
Your strengths tested, no mercy, pure anger and joy
One man, one dream ... to be the best
You do not back down on your field, your home
Rain or shine, it's on
The muddy field, brown and slippery, rainbow overhead
Chilling breezes break through your body
The heat of the moment, the goal
The sound of a heart, it's your own
The rush of adrenaline with the buzzer
Yelling and cheering, the falling and breathlessness gone
Leaping for a catch with your crosse
The sport of aggressiveness, pure talent and agility
The best of the best, a game in the spring for real men
Their pride is truly unleashed
We win
Lacrosse

Taken Away
by Lisa Santilli

He was taken away, only at three; this came as a shock to me ...
So young, not enough time to see, not enough time to be ...
With this cancer there is no cure; why are these things still so unclear?
For real this time, not with a knife; on March 21st, cancer took his life ...
Now taken away, we are left in despair, wishing we still had time to spare ...

I Hear America
by Joseph Chiusano

I hear America crying; terrorism and high gas prices
People are upset over global warming and innocent lives taken by violence
Citizens are tired of expensive heating bills with all the nations polluting the air
Money has become a big problem; people litter and don't care about it
I hear America singing for the president; the many sights of our nation
For the American flag, for the soldiers in Iraq
The soldiers that come home safely, for researchers looking for a cure for diseases
The freedom of America; singing with an open mouth its melodious songs

Shattered Soul
by Lexi Cocco

The music is loud, but sounds are silent
Raging voices, soft but violent
The world spins, the sky goes 'round
Flailing in the air, you gulp and drown
No way out, you've stumbled in
Into the fires of a stentorian din
Smashing, crashing, the world around you
The flames are doused with oceans of blue
A flutter of lashes, flashing red lights
Before everything goes the whiteness of night
You're dead, you're gone, you won't return
No matter how your dead-heart yearns
A person sighs, a small child cries
All at your very early demise
A cracked tombstone bears your name
As your apparition turns head in shame
A weeping willow tickles the stone with leafy tears
Wracked with the grief of your tender lost years
As was anyone else's prediction
You could have fought your deadly addiction

I Hear America
by Kristina Blank

I hear America crying, shedding tears for soldiers lost in war
Having moist cheeks from incurable diseases
Their eyes are red from the world's pollution
They have sore and dry throats from screaming in pain
Their hands are trembling from drug and alcohol abuse
They have deaf ears from the gunshots around them
I hear America, opening up and they're crying, telling the world of their concerns
I hear America singing, their voices are ringing with freedom
They have callused hands from the hard work of amazing opportunities
Their hearts are full of love and dedication to our country
The business suits worn to the good paying, accomplished jobs
The smiles in the advancements of technology that makes their lives easier
They are full of pride and friendships that will last to the end of their days
I hear America, full of life, and they're singing what is rightfully theirs
Singing, with open mouths, a melodious song

Sentience
by Li-Ning Yang

He touches her arm, caresses her hair; she is perfect, beautiful, pure
Untouched by selfish human desires, she is the epitome of perfection
Rapturous, awed, he gazes at her
His goddess, his heart's desire, his ideal, the perfect woman
"My goddess," he whispers fervently
He will keep her to himself, he thinks
And here, separated from the outside world by steel laboratory doors
They will build their life in paradise
Her perfection, her naivety, will absolve him of his sins
Her love, which he will receive, is the end of his meandering path
"I'll never let you go," he swears
She will be his, and his alone, his only, his perfect doll-girl, going into eternity
Over her, he will have absolute power
After all, he is her god, just as she is his goddess
"As I created you from wires, tubes, and steel, and programmed you for me"
He tells her, "You will create something for me ... "
"You," he says, "Will create my paradise"
And then, she opens her eyes

Behind Her Pretty Face
by Michele Fitzpatrick

What is the real beauty behind her attitude?
Is she trying to hide herself with a nasty mood?
What is the truth behind her pretty face?
Is she just going through another phase?
Why does she try to act so perfect?
She knows she wants to break down and cry
What is she thinking? All she wants to do is fit in
Then does she think she will win?
She's losing herself and her family
How is she ever going to get herself back?
This we will never know and that is a fact

Unbreakable Family
by Heather Vargo

All of my life, I could always see
I was treated like that porcelain precious moment no one wanted to break
I was as sensitive as a kitten, weak and frail in emotions
But I have never gone a day without feeling loved
From that soft butterfly kiss, to that huge bear hug
It was obvious our family was unbreakable
Many people are green with envy from our strong bond
Not missing any pieces to our long jigsaw puzzle we call life
Our relationships are a never ending scavenger hunt
With so many things we still have to discover
I am as anxious as a child on Christmas, to unfold the hidden secrets
To me my life is perfect, like a hard earned "A"
Knowing that our knot-tight family will never be broken

The Person I Don't Love
by Alana Qualls

The one person that I do not love
Is my annoying, hard-headed brother, Steve
He picks on me and makes fun of me
That's the one thing I do not need
Most of my friends like him
They think he's nice, funny and good looking
I hope they realize that he's eighteen and not their type
They're nice, he's not
He's the one, only one I don't love

The Girl Inside My Mind
by Christopher Bellows

We walked together, just last night, under the crimson sun
I got on one knee and asked you the question many men only dream of asking
You were so shocked, I'll never be able to get your expression out of my head
It will always be there as long as I'm up here
I'm sorry, baby, I didn't see the car; I guess I wasn't thinking about you
Please, tell our baby I love her and tell the girl inside my mind I love her, too

Consuming Fire
by Matthew Martin

It is known to be deadly so I regard it carefully, for one day it may consume us all
Endlessly, it creeps toward the wood; its fuel to consume the world
Nothing will stop it then, it will consume all in a glorious blaze
At least it would if it could just reach a little further
It warms us and we realize the danger; quickly we move the logs away
But that moment of quiet terror will always be with us
The knowledge that we could all burn at any time
The orange and yellow flames lick hungrily over the dry timber
Silently we watch and slowly I pick up the bucket
I throw water over the fire; slowly its sizzling rage dies away
All I can hear is the night wind whistling through the trees
As I slip restlessly back to sleep I wonder
What would have happened had the fire reached the wood?

The Raven and the Dove
by Jennifer Davis

Hast thou forgotten already of the Raven and the Dove?
Why, surely thou doth jest, good sir! ... What is that I hear? Thou are not jesting?
Well then, what a pity I must say that thou hast so easily forgot
How the world came to be a truelove knot of so many shades of gray
It was a chance that the Raven and the Dove met in the midsummer's sunset
And as they first gazed upon each other in that moment
They saw meaning within one another
For the Raven and the Dove's sunlit feathers new meaning
A safe haven from worlds within so peaceful a being
And the Dove's sunlight transformed the Raven's feathers once so darkly bleak
Into deep shades of purple and blue and green
The colors that the Raven had so desperately seeked
And from that day forward, the light and dark lived side by side
Creating a beautiful shade of gray
For after all, is not a color the reflection of every other shade than itself?
For the Raven and the Dove could not ever again exist alone
Their compliments were so exquisitely shown
And so thus it came to be, the strange love of the Raven and the Dove!

School
by Britani Hammond

School is a place where everyone and no one is safe
School is a place where everyone is accepted and everyone is rejected
School is a place where most can't express themselves
School is a place where no one can be odd or different
For if you are odd or different, you are odd or different by yourself
So watch what you say, do or wear
Because don't forget, you're in school
Remember to hide your true brain's beauty and talents
If you don't, people will stare
Do what you will, not what you want
Because don't forget, you're in school

Waterfall
by Amanda Rose Friedman

Water falling down
Falling down on the big rocks
Lots of shades of blue

Secluded
by Jordan Mims

The measure of a man ... integrity
The measure of a man ... sincerity
The measure of a man ... perseverance
The measure of a man ... the stature of triumph he conquers
The measure of a man ... the fabrications
That position themselves distant from the truth
The measure of a man ... the affection that generously flows
The measure of a man ... his family is what he upholds
The measure of a man ... the content of his attitude depicted demonstrates character
The measure of a man ... the protection for the future is underneath his wings
The measure of a man ... the stability of his feet deposit themselves firm
Depicts why we have men, to tackle a greater subject ... life

My Friend
by Kim Braun

Who is He? He's the man, the man nailed upon that tree
He's my hero, He's my friend; His love for us will never end
If you ask, He will forgive; in our hearts is where He lives
For us He died because we had Him crucified
He did not ask the question, why? So He then joined His father in the sky
Who is this man I'm speaking of? He's Jesus Christ, the one I love

Rising Kite
by Elena Sollazzo

The kite floated through the blue, cloudy sky
A cardinal grazing sponge-shaped clouds
With winds pushing it into a glide, only to float higher and higher
Till the red material is a rocket, eternally escalating into space
Rising till the air is too thin to carry it further
And the string is too short to allow it anymore length

That Old Brown Hound
by Jessica Weisheit

Rain running down the window, puddles on the ground
Rain running off that old, brown hound
He weeps with his tail sitting still
Waiting for his owners, looking into the windowsill
Awaiting their notice to bring him in
From the cold, it's not a sin

Life
by Irene Adamis

Life is a one-way ticket I hear
Sometimes it stinks and sometimes it's weird
I hear many people saying life is not fair
Sometimes we laugh and sometimes we cry
When we come down to it all, we're all alike
Life is like a game that you have to play
It lures you into a never-ending learning lesson
Each person is a playing piece
That goes forward and never backward
You must never back down, but back up
Don't trust the players or blame them either
It's just a game, a game called life

Bonnie Prince Charlie
by Bailey Ehr

They put the baby in the boat
And sang their soft goodbyes
They hoped that he would stay afloat
Amidst the arrow cries
They hoped their prince would come again
And slay the foe once more
And free them from this dreadful chain
For they had lost the war
They sent wee Charlie off to France
To save him from the king
Though they all kept their stance
They knew not what we would bring

Untitled
by Katie Newman

The house is knocked unconscious; I'm hunched over a notebook
With the meager, manufactured light of a clock to guide my finally woken hands
Slowly blinking numbers remind me to set them
It honestly doesn't matter much what they're supposed to say
These days, time and measurement's a sorry system
In a couple hours, I guess I'll leave my dreaming for another sleepwalk
Buried unreachably inside this daytime coma
Operating under the illusion that watching is as good as joining
Ten tolling bells later, I'm dumped at my own doorstep
A dark, diesel cloud behind me
Then oven's timer finds me unnoticeably napping through Lasagna Tuesday
Followed shortly by lights out and earnest wishes for sweet dreams
Missing the fact I've long been dormant, talking in my unconscious state
After a few slow revolutions on that grandfather in the kitchen
A torrent of thoughts recalls me to the hours I'm truly awake
I'm crouched over a notebook; the house is knocked unconscious

More Than a Label
by Taylor Jenkins

I'm more than a label, can't you see?
I'm more than a label; I can't stand when you judge me
You stand aside; you laugh and scoff
You try to disguise it with a fake, little cough
I'm more than a label; I'll prove it to you
I will disprove the conclusions you drew
I'm more than a label; do you believe me now?
When God looks at me, He sees His precious little child

Mommy's Little Girl
by Najmie Alice

Mommy's little girl is growing up
Mommy has seen her grow out of diapers; she learned how to walk and talk
Now it is the first day of school; Mommy holds her little girl's hand
And tells her everything will be alright; Mommy was always there for her little girl
When Mommy's little girl needed anything, anything at all
Mommy was there to save the day and give it to her
Mommy is like superwoman; the time grows wings and flies
Mommy's little girl is older and in high school now
Mommy realizes that her little girl is becoming a young woman
Mommy's little girl is growing up
Her little girl will spread her wings and soar into the sky
However, Mommy's little girl will always know
That she will always be Mommy's little girl

Cliff
by Heather Yeater

I'm looking over the edge; as I look down, I see the water fifty feet below
I stand up; I feel warm hands on my back; he pushes me off
I fall the whole fifty feet; I go under; I feel the current pulling me under
It feels like there's a cold wrinkly hand gripping my feet
I come back up finally beating the current
To find myself in my neighborhood swimming pool
He points and laughs at me; he's not paying attention; I get out of the water
Coming up behind him, I push him off the cliff!

The Greatest Gift
by Tevyn Wethington

When I think of Heaven
A remembrance of seven appears
There are seven days in a week
Which allow me to reach my peak
When I think of my papaw, sweet music comes to mind
My time with him was always fine
We shared lots of love and laughs
But you and others couldn't begin to know the other half
There will never be another love like this
But to sum it all up, it's the greatest gift

My Life
by Justina Rodado

I am from a soft and comfy couch where great memories are born
From a warm beautiful fire lit beneath the mantle
From the kittens that come to cuddle, purr and love
And the television that lights the room with excitement and joy for hours on end
I am from rooms where candles are lit and peace and serenity are found
I am from the city that never sleeps, the rushing cars and the beeps
From the Statue of Liberty standing tall with the flame of freedom
From where the towers proudly stood until that one fateful day
And where the ball drops annually and everyone counts down
I am from state of suburban towns to rural cities
I am from New York City to the California west coast
From the Grand Canyon and the Appalachian Mountains
From the happiest places on earth, Disney World and Disney Land
And where Las Vegas casinos never rest and Seattle never sleeps
I am from country where Death Valley lies and the Red Forest is and always will be
I am from the giant, impenetrable Castle El Morro
From the huge El Yunque rain forest with all it's natural beauty
From the beating hot sun that gives you such a great tan
And Old San Juan, where you can see everything great about this historical place
I am from a heritage of beautiful beaches that warm your feet and your heart

Sir
by Elizabeth Litzinger

The beating of his heart grew faint
Tears rolled down my face like a waterfall not willing to stop
Around me, sorrow filled the room
Emotions buzzing around me like bees, stinging my every movement
The room grew dark, with only a strip of light shining
Down on his cold, motionless face
Time seemed to stop
The wind stopped
The crying stopped
His heart stopped
- Dedication to my grandfather (Sir)

Strength
by Ariel Perez

Alone in the distance you stand out in the crowd
You are independent and strong, you are different and unique
And that is what sets you apart from all that's around you
You stand tall and beautiful, you have strength

Rain
by Stephanie Metal

I love the rain as it mixes with the tears streaming down my face
It hides me and my feelings, and I have something to blame it on
Not just another, but myself who needs to change
I wait, but for what?
The sun is never coming, no matter for how long you look
So go to sleep, and maybe in the morning the rain will be just a dream
I hate the rain; it gives too many places to hide
Never really letting you see the sun I miss
Where has she gone? I do believe she took my happiness with her

I Don't Know What To Do!
by Autumn Mack

I don't know what to do
I don't have a clue
Should I count all my shoes?
Should I sing the blues?
Oh, what should I do?
My mother is flying
My father is crying
Oh no, what should I do?
I can't even think
I can't find a link
To what I should do
I need something new
Maybe I could plant flowers
Or sing a new song
The extent of my powers
Is not very strong
Oh, what should I do?
I don't have a clue

So Called Friends
by Vanessa Ontiveros

They'll be your friends; they'll be with you when you're sad
You say, "I have to stop," but they say, "Stop tomorrow"
That tomorrow never comes and there is nothing else to feel but sorrow
You find help but inside, they're still there, calling you to come back
Before you know it, you're back with those friends
Those friends will turn to foes when you realize they took away your real friends
If you try to leave them, you won't have anyone
You'll see them daily; soon, you will feel bad, unnatural
Those friends will take your life
That's when you regret the day you met them
Those drugs, your so called "friends"
Will look for someone like you, gullible and weak
Waiting for their new friends to take the same steps as you did

Why?
by Sean Hatfield

We ask ourselves why; why can't we trust one another?
Why do we always mess things up when we are with each other?
Why can't we know the true meaning of love?
Why do we always sink below and never rise above?
Why do our so called friends talk behind our back?
Why do we think this and feel like we're about to snap?
Why can't we just turn the bad things around?
Why do we always turn our smiles upside down?
Why do we always argue and fight?
Why can't we stop this and just make things right?
Why do we have to listen to all these lies?
We both know it's way too soon to say our goodbyes

Gymnastics
by Kylie Crawford

Gymnastics is an awesome sport!
It's long winters with cold, short summers with hot
A gymnast's work can never stop
It's chalky palms with grips, it's vault with nine six
It's floor with leos up your butt, it's beam with a sharp pain in your gut!
Sweaty palms, chalky grips, lose your balance, once you tripped
Floor is a blast, beams a test, bars goes by fast and after vault you need rest!
Though a gymnast will cry once or twice on their way
They will always be brave and work harder for the next day
This test you see is quiet a lot to cope
And to do this sport you must have hope!
Even through all the torments, always remember that
Today's training is tomorrow's performance!

My Mind
by Jorden Bonney

I sit here in the middle of the night
Day after day crying because I'm thinking of only you
The good times, the bad times, the times we spent together
The more I thought about you, the more it made me cry
I couldn't stop thinking about you; I can't stop thinking about you
You're the only one on my mind; I try to talk to you but the words won't come out
It's like I ate a whole jar of peanut butter because I can't talk
When I see you, I cry and freeze up and when your name is mentioned
Tears form at the bottom of my eyes
I broke your heart and mine in the process, too
So what I'm trying to say is, I love you!

It's the Truth
by Nicholas Sesto

My homework is late
Why, forgot to check the date?
My computer broke
Did it have a stroke?
Grandma is sick
Did she get bit by a tick?
Grandpa has a disease
Was he attacked by bees?
I was studying my abc's
I know, you were stung by fleas!
There was this really huge tree
It collapsed and sprained your knee?
My homework blew up
So, that's what's up?
My homework died
It's ok, I know you cried

So Sad For My Dad
by Lucus Mills

Something terrible happened to my dad, he died
It was on a hot sunny day when he passed away
I wanted to go to my room and just hide
Instead we went to lay flowers on his grave today
I tried so hard to get my dad out of my mind
Once in a great while, I get lots of tears
You can die at a drop of a dime at anytime
I hope something like that doesn't happen again for many years
Sometimes I just want to go cry in my bed
There was a picture of my dad on the wall and the wind made it fall
I go to bed with my dad in my head
The next day it was sunny
I took all the stuff out of my mind and then I had fun
But one thing I didn't forget was that I invested all his money

What the World Owes Me
by Trevor Hartman

The world owes me parents; I don't know why God took them from me
I now feel lost inside; I don't know how God couldn't see
That since they've gone, I'm all alone without my mom and dad
I wish they were here but they're not, and that makes me very sad
I feel inhuman without my parents, for parents are here to love
My dad is now in prison, but my mom is up above
My family is still here and they are not yet to pack
I miss my parents oh so much; the world owes me my parents back

That Day
by KaLyn Franchini

Beaten and bruised, cut with cruelty, harshly tried with no way out
He did not plead innocent, though guilty He was not
Carrying a cross alongside seventy times seven trillion sins
To the Mount of Olives; death waited
Nails that could not spiritually hold Him there; physically clutched to the cross
Lots cast for His clothes; ridiculed with no mercy
Humility latched Him to the cross
"Father forgive them for they know not what they do"
His last breath, spear in His side, the blood of love spilled out
Three days passed and He arose, coming back in full form
For you and me, Jesus died and arose

Escape
by Leslee Henderson

I let out a sigh
As I look to the sky
I wonder how long this beauty will last
The world always changes so fast
The grass beneath me is so lush
From far away the city is hushed
Nothing but nature is what I hear
A trickling stream is very near
My eyes squint as they see the sun
Butterflies fly, as though it was fun
For a moment I see
The little squirrel in the tree
Soon to be scared away by a bird
Rustling leaves is what is left to be heard
Pretty birds chirp and sing a song
The sun won't be out for very long
I pack up my blanket and head for my car
From where I am to my house, it won't be far
As the light turns to dark
I leave the park
I leave my escape

3rd
Place

Victoria Barker

Victoria is an avid reader, has a 4.0 GPA
and is a proud member of the National Junior Honor Society.
Captain of her school's Parliamentary Procedures Team,
this eighth grade poet is also involved in FFA,
recently winning a state competition in food science.
She attends youth group at church
and enjoys swimming in her spare time.

Remembering
by Victoria Barker

They sit motionless
Pieces of their silver hair sparkle in the light
The gray bonnets are tied around their heads
As if to cover the painful memories that still ring clear in their minds
Occasionally the rocking chair squeaks, but neither one seems to notice
Nothing can break them from this trance
They are too busy remembering how great everything was
Horrific scenes race through their minds
It's hard to forget all the red flashing lights
On that rainy Christmas Eve
As the sun begins to set over the hill, they get up
It will be time for supper soon

Reba Shields

This talented ninth grade student
loves poetry, music, and especially animals.
In fact, one day Reba hopes to fulfill her dream
of becoming a veterinarian.
For now, she divides her time between FCCLA
and the Drama Club at her school
where she is also a member of the Honor Roll Society.

Split 6
by Reba Shields

How to explain the woes of a child
Who must talk to herself everyday
To compensate all of the people
Who invade and conquer her mind
There are five other selves behind her
And each gets their own moment to shine
When sharing a body with six
It's like a full house with no room to breathe
The worst part of all is the truth
She knows and created each one
But a game went wrong and now she goes on
In a shell of six different personas
Three boys and three girls make up herself
Each one the opposite of another
The twins, the actor, the friend, cousin and shadow
All make up the one little girl
"It's easier than thought," she says to me
It's like we all live in the same world
The twins know the actor; the actor, the shadow
And there is no room for alone

Devin Harris

While reading and drawing
are some of Devin's favorite activities,
it is a passion for writing
which truly defines this eighth grade student.
In fact, becoming a published writer
is said to have been a life-long ambition.
We are now pleased to provide this opportunity
for an author whom we feel is genuinely gifted.

The White Dragon
by Devin Harris

A thousand radiant white lights
Each one a shining scale
Lay upon its body
Like a suit of sparkling mail
A row of gleaming diamond spikes
Bristle on its tail
Its wings are spun with pure moonlight
Each one a frosted sail
An agile creature of the air
Its body slim and lithe
Its fangs are ivory daggers
Each claw, a crystal scythe
It breathes a cloud of milk-white flames
Into the pitch-black night
And soars across the starry skies
A captivating sight

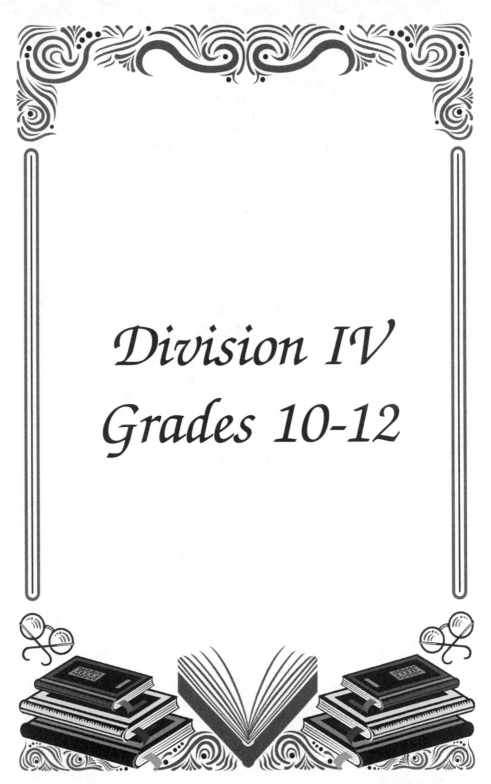

Division IV
Grades 10-12

Pop
by Ashley Bender

Drip, drop, plink, plop, that's the sound of tears
Tears of a friend who watched you drink a few too many beers
Tears of a friend who watched you as you left the bar
Tears of a friend who watched you as you got in the car
Tears of a friend who watched you crash
Tears of a friend who saw your body upon the dash
Tears of a friend who heard the car whine
Tears of a friend who wishes to turn back time
Tears of a friend who could not look
Tears of a friend who signed your yearbook
Tears of a friend who saw the cop
Tears of a friend who said, "Why couldn't we have just drank pop?"

Snowflake
by Kelly Fleming

The cold can singe her skirts, and the wind can howl her away
But she is a single flaw, falling, waning in bursts
Kissing the air raw in her white sylph-like dress
Frayed in her lovely hurt, she faints alone, always

Venezia
by Jung Hee Choi

I lived in a town called the mecca of corruption
Abandoned by God, everything was left behind
There thou came, whispered love softly but with a passion
Thy smile put me in a misty dream where peacefully lives a hind
Thou, as my small wing, learned how to hope and fly for the first time
Even though I had a punishment like gouging my heart
Could not see the reality clearly when my eyes blocked by sweet rime
So me against destiny, eagerly wanted thou, drew thou on my piece of art
But the one and only love betrayed me; such event no one ever expected
My wing torn apart, thrown away, me strangled to death
Wandering around night streets with hunger, being suffocated
Yet in my dream, happily with thee I laid down on Earth
Arms and legs broken by thou, but have my own wings now
Grown up, without thee, I fly away from the callous town and row

Long But Short
by Sergio Guess

My life will be long but time will make it short
I will live it strong but time will build its fort
Like walking into a trap, it consumes its prey
As my life is devoured and killed by times of delay
My body will soon rot and decay
But time will renew itself everyday
Life for me is like a journey beyond control
But in the end, time will selfishly take its toll
It is like a bleak foreshadow of what lies ahead
Being wasted and thrown away, like a molded piece of bread
I feel like a bag of grain being emptied by the pound
Emptying until there's nothing to be found

After a Storm
by Rena Richards

The lightning strikes, the rain pours
The thunder crashes, everyone is indoors
The sun peeks out, the rain slows
The clouds depart, a rainbow shows
The grass glows, the sky is light
The air flows, flowers are bright
The animals play, the day is warm
The world is gay after a storm

Walking Through a Place
by Gary Tarantino

The night was dark and gloomy
With not even the presence of the homeless on the sidewalks of the city streets
It was 3 a.m. and the man just got out of work
With just a briefcase and cup of coffee in hand
The man was surrounded by the bright lights of the downtown area
Taxis passed as if they were in a rush as mid-day
Disregarding the hand signal of the lonely worker
So there the man walked another 18 blocks to his apartment on 85th and Columbus
A walk that will take him 33 minutes

Truth
by Michael Rodd

As a son, I lost a father
As a friend, I lost a friend
If the choice was mine, I'd rather none
I know you're there, but where to go?
Only one could choose my way
Help me pass this test of life and get to you
To rule as one, as a son, as a friend
Both are missed each and everyday
A goal is made to reach that way
Way of living you taught so well
I make a promise to stay and pray that one day
I'll meet with you to chase the pain away

Lion's Roar
by Christian Ang

Old, stale depression, like the possession of the soul
Gnawing the threads of will inside the inner being
Supposedly the lion's roar, projectile screams so shrill
Entirely followed by the howling, the calls at the moon
With the bloodcurdling screams of the obsession
Writhing through nerves, right to the deranged brain
Look into a trench of despair and find that light
Seems impossible to figure out the meaning of life
Mission complete, finish by riding the train of doom
Agony clutching to that glass heart and shattering it all
Mere thoughts of defeat and destruction just keep laughing
Laughing the reasons why it tries to claw us down to Hell
Have you see it yet, the depression's the disease
Someone needs help to diffuse that impending ignition
Revulsion in the soul when you defy the help of friends
They worry their minds off for that one again and again
Three years have sung a tune that I eventually forgot
I got a letter in the mail on that yellow-skied, rainy day
The lion is dead, the lion is dead, the lion chose death instead
Whereabouts unknown, empty shell, the lion took its fall

Wolf Self
by Lea Brinkman

A secret part of me
Many don't know, nor will understand
A reflection of myself; in a different view
A self of which I wish to tell
Yet, it's my safe-kept secret; a wolf self, I treasure
With a dreadful past of pain and broken hearts
But a future that's been brightening each and every day
The comfort of family and friends, even children of my own
All of them; I wish and hope no harm comes
I cherish what I've found and refuse to give it up
To the shadows of the past

You Mean Everything To Me
by Merissa Haynes

You mean everything to me because you're not just anything
You are something and when I see you face to face, all it does is hit home base
I hit the ball and run! Pitcher makes the next move as I hit first base
All of a sudden, I hear the crowd stop; stuck there, I stand and watch
As he picks up the bat, he walks up there and says, "Throw it fast!"
Strike one ... I watch him think it through; what did I do?
Strike two ... he couldn't figure it out, then I watch you strike out
I hear the disappointment in the crowd as you walk to the dug out
You say, "Guys, I'm sorry I lost this game"
I watch you walk away; I'm still stuck in time as he rewinds
All of a sudden, we're both in a different place
I'm tired of being ignored; I gave up because my hope failed to stay
Heartbroken and confused, I asked myself, "What did I do?"
Then I stopped to think; I did nothing because I thought you were my everything
When I watched you walk away, I'd really hope you'd stay
Tears drop as I sit down and pray for this to all stop
Wished you'd fast forward and meet me up because you're not just nothing
You are something, you're more than anything, you were my everything
My fear was losing you; step back and take a breath as I hope for the best
Still wish you'd sit and stay, talk to me in that certain way
Like a rose, the petals drop as I watch you walk; I tried to make that home run!
Struck out; I tried to meet you up; didn't feel the same when I saw you face to face
I tried to rewind, but didn't do it quiet in time
So step up to that plate; tell me, please, what's your wait?
Still feel the same about you; now just hope you do too!
Because you are still everything to me

Life-Size
by Eric Hatt

Blind to cries, hearing lies; hear something new
It's something we all adore, something called the truth
It's recognized as a nursery rhyme; this all may sound crude
But the change you're bringing, the call you're singing
Is brought by the axe you use
A question remains as to why you ignore; is it all simply for pride?
Since when was pride the new fad? Are you still on the inside?
Do you fear to learn that you caused this, a tear from the world's cheek?
Bringing the vows on honeymoon days, to last only a week
Or is it the change you fear? Ah yes, the change, the start of this new lore
The new days have felt so safe to you; you must lose what you adore
Why dread this? A scratch on stone, one less star at night
Dare to move; try something new; change from death to life

In This Place That Makes Things Happen
by Arielle Glash

Through the eyes of the beholder, the color pink appears
Showing the fluster of one's emotions and the bubbly explosions that occur
Through the eyes of the mother, the color red appears
Showing the anger and frustration that is engaged in the altercation of the two
Through the eyes of the father, the color blue appears
Showing the drowning of sorrow that deepens as the years go on
The tension and troubles that occur have forever been forgotten
In this place that makes things happen
Butterflies swim and fish could fly, as the lions hop and the turtles run by
People are nice to one another and no one's dream would be smothered
The music plays and never ends
Though the roads could bend in a way that feels comfortable
And one can tilt their head
The tension and troubles that occur have forever been forgotten
In this place that makes things happen
Through the eyes that belong to me, the world appears
Showing the creation of love, imagination and life
In my head, everything can become a reality and this is the only place for me to be

Just Do It, Just Do It
by Kiya Freels

Ok, I have so many feelings to let out; am I too skinny or too stout?
Just do it, just do it
Will I ever see my daddy again, or will my endless sea of tears never end?
Just do it, just do it
Can I ever talk to my mom, or find a good man to take to the prom?
Just do it, just do it
Time to let go full throttle; I can't keep these feelings kept up in a bottle
Just do it, just do it
I feel full of sins, stress and doubt, it's time to just do it and let these feelings out!
Just do it, just do it

Typical City Morning
by Anthony Esposito

On my brand new twenty-one speed Schwinn, I rode
I rode through the smog
Which fills the body with the beautiful vapor of a city skyline
I rode past a fire hydrant where a bum had just relieved himself
I rode past the playground
Where the swing seats were clammy from the morning dew
I rode past a child, a petite, blonde girl who claimed her bike had been stolen
And so ... I walked

Rest In Peace Mark and Drew
by Kaylee Kemp

You never knew that I loved you and now you never will
There was nothing I could say or do; in the ground you lay so still
Two kids is what you used to be, letting the wind blow in your hair
Somehow, I feel you close to me, protecting me through the air
I cried for so long when they told me that night
I never found a single song that made it be alright
I guess I didn't know you that great; I really wish that I did
Most people now only show the hate; I loved you so much that I only hid
I know that you are having fun, hanging out with Drew
While we are down here, up until we're done, we all really do love you

Winter In the Woods
by Laura Rossano

The sky is a pink rose, the snow is a blanket
The trees are soldiers, waiting for commands
The bare and jagged branches are wizard wands
Zapping the sky for more snow to come
The landscape sleeps; more snow falls
It is winter in the woods

A Father Never Known
by Adam McGriff

Even prior to light, while still in my shell
We left you behind, did I miss heaven or hell?
The path that was chosen was rocky and warped
But I'm happy enough, though my hand was dealt short
This void was never noticed, I've never needed it filled
Those absent cards I never miss, toward you I feel no ill
So live your life that is your own, and I will do the same
Both of us have rolled the dice, we're just playing different games

Young and Naive
by Megan Jones

Thought you were my friend, maybe I judged by the cover before I read the book
So much education, yet so naive; immaturity dwells in the depths of me
Blinded by appearances ... oblivious to the soul intentions that lie beneath
You played me like dominoes; then used me like a battery and threw me out
But my package says rechargeable so you're the one who missed out
You smiled in my face and shoved daggers in my back
Who could betray their own friend? You meddled in my life
Took happiness from me with one touch of your poisonous hands
Your actions were evil but in my eyes, evil never wins!
I'm glad I realized trust is overrated, so, who can I run to?
I pity those who stab their friends in the back
They are the ones who are young and naive
Young and naive was once me but ... Young and naive they will always be!

Freak
by Michele Meshover

I step into cement cubes connected by grey grout
And plastered on parallel, wide walls
Flickering, fluorescent lights flash in unison with my pace
Twelve inch tiles show their bland and palpable patterns
Scuff marks and dry, mud footprints left behind from those who walked before us
Their gathering, glacial stares dart in my direction
Like I am a murderer, rebel or thief
And stab me straight in the eye with an arrowhead
For others, a glance my way is a waste of their precious time
Because I am an alien, freak and creep
And their bodies pass me by with no acknowledgment, like frigid winter winds
While stuck inside a transparent bubble
My hand grazes the soapy barrier and I struggle to carry on once again
With one poke by a gentle hand, I would be released from my sealed covering
But the people clear and I am left alone
Still stuck, still vanishing into the quicksand tiles

The Storm
by Samantha Pearson

Birth is like a storm
As we feel the warmth of our mother's hand
Like the first raindrop falls to the ground
As we get older, we start to play with a ball
We start to hear a little rumble
As we get older, a strike of lightning
Strikes like a news flash screaming for attention
As we became an adult, it starts to rain a little bit harder
As we open our eyes, life has gotten harder than we think
The storm has gotten stronger; we just stepped into parenthood
As we hear our children yelling and screaming down the hall
We hear the rumble in the sky getting louder and louder
A lightning strikes again showing us that our kids
Have moved on with their lives
The storm is coming to an end
As we remember all these memories
It's about our time to go, as well as the storm's

At the End of It All, Maybe There Is Hope
by James Rudis

All the rage, even compassion cannot save
As the burnt gray smoke surrounds me, chokes me
All the hate in the world laughs, smirks
Gathering its discrimination, its prejudice
Until that's all there is, all the pain, all the rage
Yet, I can't stop it, contain it; killings, hateful eyes watching, waiting
Wrath controlling us, consuming us like shadows in darkness
War rages on, hate spreads; carnage it brings; there's no hope
I watch this like a Greek statue, violence in their arguments
Oh! Why can't I stop it? Is there anyway to stop it?
No! I think the hate is in us all and we can never let it go; how hard we try
As the burnt smoke surrounding me fades away, I think
As I close my eyes, the bombs overhead gather
Maybe there's hope; at the end of it all, maybe there's hope

Emily Stacken
by Kelsey Lesher

I was only twenty eight when I died
I worked at the local school in town
I was a counselor for young children with problems
I made young kids' lives better or so I thought
One day, I walked in my office when I noticed Toby
A third grade boy sitting in my chair
Toby had many problems at home with his parents
The two of us spent days talking about his problems together
Until one day, Toby walked in my office but it wasn't his time to talk
He told me he had a surprise to give me
But as usual, I didn't think anything of it
Until he reached in his pocket to pull something out
The last thing I heard was two gunshots
One for me and one for young Toby

Love's Call
by Jessica Nelson

I am dancing in my lover's arms
I am dancing in my place of solitude
In my place of paradise
Where is this place you wonder?
Where am I, you ask?
Beyond these walls created by misfortune and pain
Is where I danced the carols of the discordant
And touch the sweet fragrance of my Creator's words
Upon a new arrival of day
He whispers, "I made this place for you"
"For what is more wonderful than you?"
"You are mine," He whispers, "I created you"
The roaring waves are silenced by His call
The sound of my Keeper is honeysuckle on my lips
The crashes of spring colors threaten my breath
One said, many years ago
"Do not awaken love until it so desires"
I tell you now, accept the hand before you
The one who loves you and calls you His
Is asking you to dance with Him

I Am From Doves
by Katherine Mahan

I am from doves
Love on my wings and beautiful songs in my heart; I try to call out
My beak is muzzled; my wings are broken
No longer can I sing; no longer can I breathe
One out of so many can not be noticed, acting like a leech
Crows begin to circle me; cawing and flapping their wings
Winter begins ... Snow falls ... Crows fade ... Sun disappears
Flying blindly in a shell
No snakes

Disheartening
by Molly Rice

The torch shined bright
Upon that very spot
Where the light
Was never sought
No matter the season
Nor the time of day
We all look for reason
To escape a fray
The heart is fragile
This I state
We are all susceptible
Because of fate

Hope
by Robin Reynolds

Hope is the color of a new sun
Hope is whispers to God for help
Hope tastes like the purest water
Hope is the smell of the sweetest wildflowers in the forest
Hope is a lighted candle in a corner of a dark house
Hope is laughter and tears of the loneliest people
Hope is the color of the brightest, white cloud in the sky
Hope is the sound of angels singing for lost souls
Hope tastes of fresh strawberries by a hidden waterfall
Hope is the smell of honeysuckle by a lake sparkling like diamonds
Hope is walking through a quiet garden
Hope is loving someone who will never love you
Hope is the color of stars that shine at night
Hope is the sound of a thousand winds that blow
Hope tastes of ripe apples just fallen from the apple tree
Hope smells of a fire in a dark night
Hope is someone leaving footprints on your heart
Hope is a reminder that anything is possible
Hope is a cloudy night with the moonlight shining through

Our Dreams
by Kassandra Sterritt

I've got dreams as big as the stars
I like to put my makeup on and go work on cars
They say you're a different kind of girl
And you're never going to make it in this grown up world
They say I'm as wild and unruly as the summer wind
That no matter how hard I try, I will always wind up where I begin
My pride just doesn't let me give in; fighting for your dream to come true isn't a sin
Don't get me wrong, I've been knocked down a time or two
And I know what it's like to put my heart back together with Super Glue
Somehow I'm still making it through; it's what I was born to do
Most people see this fire in my eyes and wonder how I always know just what to do
I believe in myself and I believe in you
I've seen dreams fall apart that have never come true, and now they never can
Friend, give me a chance and believe in me
I'll be there holding your hand, proving to this broken down, knocked around world
That we can stand on our own and bring our dreams on home

Could Be
by Stephanie Owens

Nothing is important, just take me out
I don't want to be in your life when you are going to hate and shout
Nothing is important, cut me off
Exclude me from your drama if you are just going to save it for another scoff
Nothing is important, so why lie?
Friendship apparently means nothing to you, so I am leaving with just a goodbye
Nothing is important, I am sick of the stabs
You went past your limit, I am going to die from the jabs
Nothing is important, now here is your last chance
Friend or foe, 'cause I could be gone in a glance

3rd
Place

Pamela Lé Sant

Pamela is a senior in high school
and has earned honors in English and History.
She has sharpened her writing skills
working with the school newspaper,
and is also an honored member of Student Council.
Her heart however, belongs to children in need,
and it is for this reason that she has chosen a career path in Pediatrics.

Without
by Pamela Lé Sant

Gone is the music which drove me
The tune, lost on the wind's breath
Misused, mislaid, misplaced
Flown are the notes that conducted the rhythms
The song danced so easily with different beats
Marches of the long dull days
Jazz rips during wanton nights
The soothing sonnets and sleepy lullabies of brandies and breakfasts
A strayed strain of abandoned love
Left is only emptiness
No ruined harmonies or unfinished opuses
But motifs, no longer heard, only remembered
In a prison of silence

Adam Pliskin

We are not the first to recognize Adam's literary skills.
This eleventh grade honor student not only serves as Editor of the
school newspaper, but contributes to its literary magazine as well.
In addition to playing the guitar, he is an up-and-coming filmmaker
who plans on pursuing a career in the motion picture industry.

Warriors of Ruin
by Adam Pliskin

And we roll on
Past the drums that beat us back to the cacophony of our youth
Down the wistful hills of yesterday
The winding roads that carve
The fragile outline of meandering memories
To the time-torn, decaying docks
Where ghosts stare into the tide of the past
Imparting their arcane knowledge on the waves
To the horizon line
The place where sun tastes ocean's salty breath upon its lips
And then bows its ancient head below the sullen sea
Where we cast our forgotten dreams like glassy stones
Never to rise again
And we roll on along the path of reckless nostalgia
Warriors of ruin

1st
Place

Steven Abel

When he is not writing award winning poetry,
this high school senior entertains
as an accomplished musician in his high school jazz band.
In addition to the saxophone,
Steven has mastered the guitar, keyboard, and bass,
and even plays with local bands when school is out.
He is also active in politics
and serves as president of the school political group he founded.
The America Library of Poetry is pleased to present
"Sonnet For Everyday People" by Steven Abel,
this year's Editor's Choice Award Winner.

Editor's Choice Award

Sonnet For Everyday People
by Steven Abel

The business world, it sits atop its throne
And all those left in holes below look up
With callused hands and feet scraped down to bone
They envy those who drink from Greed's Gold Cup
Please recognize what businessmen produce
In minds of men, they craft want into need
And still we all hold on to this abuse
Despite the Wars for Oil that they let bleed
I'm not a demographic; I am real
I feel for farmer's crops and doctor's drugs
While homeless women pray for their next meal
A businessman decides on Persian rugs
We idolize the rich and their champagne
And find the miracles of life mundane

Index

of

Authors

•••

Index of Authors

Index of Authors

Index of Authors

Index of Authors

With Honors
Price List

Initial Copy..................................32.95

Additional Copies......................... 24.00

*Please Enclose $6 Shipping/Handling Each Order

Check or Money Order Payable to:

The America Library of Poetry
P.O. Box 978
Houlton, Maine 04730

Must specify book title and author

Please Allow 21 Days For Delivery

THE AMERICA
LIBRARY OF POETRY

www.libraryofpoetry.com
Email: generalinquiries@libraryofpoetry.com

Poetry On the Web

See Your Poetry Online!

This is a special honor reserved exclusively for our published poets.

Now that your work has been forever set in print,
why not share it with the world at www.libraryofpoetry.com

At the America Library of Poetry,
our goal is to showcase quality writing in such a way
as to inspire others to broaden their literary horizons,
and we can think of no better way to reach people around the world
than by featuring poetic offerings like yours on our global website.

Since we already have your poem in its published format,
all you need to do is copy the information from the form below on
a separate sheet of paper, and return it with a $6 posting fee.
This will allow us to display your poetry
on the internet for one full year.

Author's Name _____

Poem Title _____

Book Title _____ *With Honors* _____

Mailing Address _____

City _____ State _____ Zip Code_____

Check or Money Order in the amount of $6 payable to:
The America Library of Poetry
P.O. Box 978
Houlton, Maine 04730